MAKING THE CONNECTION

5 SIMPLE WAYS TO BUILD COMMUNICATION AND INTERACTION WITH YOUR CHILD WITH AUTISM

MORGAN STONE

CONTENTS

INTRODUCTION

As the soft morning sunlight poured through the window, John and Sarah sat quietly in their small, cozy living room, their fingers intertwined. They'd spent the past hour in silence, merely watching their two-year-old son, Alex. His beautiful blue eyes were focused intently on his favorite toy —a colorful spinning top that he would twist with an uncharacteristic precision for his age. He was fully absorbed in his own world, oblivious to his surroundings.

This wasn't how John and Sarah had imagined their mornings would be with their firstborn. In their dreams, they had pictured laughter-filled rooms, Alex running around with boundless energy, and constant chatter about the world through a toddler's eyes. But their reality was strikingly different. Alex seldom made eye contact, rarely responded to his name, and demonstrated an unusual fascination with particular objects. His world was unique, uncharted—a puzzle they were yet to piece together.

The journey of parenthood, they knew, was not without its challenges. But the sheer quietness of their mornings, the absence of Alex's laughter, and the vacuum created by his unresponsiveness made them realize—there was a challenge they hadn't quite anticipated. And when the diagnosis finally came, their fear was given a name: Autism Spectrum Disorder (ASD).

The news was a paradigm shift in their lives. Suddenly, they found themselves lost in a labyrinth of doctor visits, therapy sessions, and a deluge of information about autism. From understanding the symptoms to uncovering the most effective intervention strategies, the diagnosis was overwhelming and nerve-wracking, a continuous test of their emotional and mental resilience.

Their story could very well be your story. Like John and Sarah, you might be at a crossroads. Caught in the shock of an ASD diagnosis, bombarded by a plethora of information, and grappling with a deep-seated fear of the unknown. You might feel desperate, lonely, and uncertain about what to do next. The unspoken questions hang heavy in the air - What now? How do I connect with my child? How can I best support their development? How do I navigate this new world of ASD?

It's a familiar tale for parents who have recently learned that their child has autism. The immediate aftermath of diagnosis is often marked by a whirlwind of emotions—shock, denial, anger, grief. The process is daunting, and you're likely trying to keep afloat amidst the storm.

But it's important to remember—you're not alone. And it's okay to feel overwhelmed. It's okay to feel scared. Because underneath that fear is an underlying love for your child—a love that propels you to seek answers, embrace the challenge, and embark on a journey that might be difficult but is by no means impossible. That's what this book is for—to guide you through this journey, one step at a time.

This book presents you with an easy-to-follow, 5-step strategy for connecting with your child on a profound level. Years of extensive research and personal experiences from countless parents who walked this path before you have been distilled into this practical guide. You will find heartwarming success stories like Alex, who started to engage more with his surroundings and even say a few words, or Emily, who learned to make eye contact and interact socially, thanks to the strategies described in this book.

These aren't miracles, but results of parents who decided to take the plunge and learn to navigate this world, just like you are about to do. These stories show that a positive, meaningful change can happen, helping you envision a future where you are not just coping but thriving as a parent of a child with ASD.

This book doesn't claim to offer a quick fix or a one-size-fits-all solution, but it will guide you along your path with actionable steps and valuable tips. The journey might be challenging, but remember, you are not alone. And while the road to understanding ASD may seem daunting, there is hope and a wealth of knowledge available to support you. We hope this guide will illuminate your path, providing clarity, hope, and reassurance.

You might be thinking, "Is this the right book for me?" If you've just started on this journey and are looking for practical guidance on connecting with your child who has just been diagnosed with ASD, then the answer is a resounding yes.

John and Sarah, like many parents who have just received an ASD diagnosis for their child, were suddenly thrust into a world they had little knowledge of. They found themselves scrolling through endless articles about the common symptoms of autism in toddlers, trying to understand where Alex fit in.

They learned that their son's fascination with spinning objects, his unusual focus, was a common characteristic of ASD. His inability to make eye contact, his lack of response when called, his struggle with using gestures—these were all markers they'd unknowingly overlooked. Reading about them was like slowly lifting the veil off a mystery that had been playing out right before their eyes.

But with every piece of information they uncovered, more questions arose. Were they doing enough to support Alex's development? How would they navigate the unfamiliar terrain of therapies, special educators, and healthcare professionals? Each article and resource, while informative, seemed to magnify their anxieties. It was like standing before an ocean, unsure of how to cross it.

Their emotional turmoil was a mixture of reactions. They oscillated between disbelief and acceptance, hope and despair, anger and guilt. They were mourning the life they had envisioned for their son while trying to gather the strength to face reality.

And looming above everything else was the pressure to act quickly. The emphasis on early intervention weighed heavy on their hearts. They'd read about studies showing that early and intensive intervention could significantly improve a child's development.

This flurry of emotions, this pressure to act while processing the new reality, this overwhelming tide of information—is this how you feel too? If your story mirrors that of John and Sarah's, know it's natural to feel overwhelmed, scared, and confused. It's okay to have a myriad of questions and to be unsure of the next step. This book is your hand-held guide to navigating these choppy waters, to find answers, and to create a path that will help your child and your family.

When you picked up this book, it wasn't the title or cover design that drew you in; it was something much deeper, an unspoken urgency that resonated within you. Perhaps, just like John and Sarah, you've found yourself at a crossroads where you're balancing the initial shock and emotional turmoil of the ASD diagnosis with the immediate need to act.

Maybe your catalyst was when you noticed your child struggling with social interactions, their difficulty in sharing emotions, or their distinctive behavior patterns that set them apart from their peers. Perhaps it was the day the doctor confirmed your fears with a diagnosis of autism or the first time you felt the gnawing worry of how you could help your child navigate this complex world.

Your catalyst might have been that overwhelming flood of information and advice you've received from every corner —professionals, well-meaning family members, friends, internet articles—leaving you with more questions than answers. The sudden realization of how different your parenting journey will be compared to others might have been the trigger.

Or it could have been the understanding that time is of the essence—that early intervention can shape your child's future, and the earlier you start, the better. The knowledge that every second is precious and that your actions today can make a profound difference in your child's life tomorrow.

The truth is, we all have different triggers, but they stem from the same deep-rooted desire: the longing to do the best for our children, to equip them with the tools they need, and to ensure they lead fulfilling lives, no matter the challenges ahead. This book is a response to that catalyst, to that call to action. It's an understanding nod to your worries and fears and a promise to guide you through your challenges—offering practical, accessible, and effective strategies to connect with your child in the earliest stages of their life.

There's an old saying: "The journey of a thousand miles begins with a single step." That step for you may be holding this book in your hands. It's a daunting journey, no doubt, but here's the good news: This book will not merely be your companion; it will serve as your compass.

Inside these pages, you'll discover a unique approach tailored specifically for parents like you—those whose path has taken an unexpected detour into the realm of autism. The benefits you'll gain from reading this book are numerous and transformative.

Firstly, it offers you simplicity. In a sea of complex and often contradictory information, this 5-step strategy is one of clarity. It's straightforward, practical, and easy to follow. It focuses on what truly matters—building a deep, meaningful connection with your child from the earliest stages.

Each step is designed to guide you in understanding your child's unique world and learning practical ways to communicate and bond with them. These steps are not mere theories but actionable insights that you can incorporate into your everyday routine, turning ordinary moments into opportunities for connection and growth.

You'll also learn how to navigate the maze of therapy options and education plans, advocate for your child's needs, and cultivate a supportive community. The strategies will empower you to make informed decisions and ensure your child gets the necessary support.

Moreover, this book will provide you with shortcuts. Imagine bypassing the overwhelming amount of information online and receiving tried and tested methods instead. This book gives you that. It's the distillation of years of professional expertise and first-hand experiences of parents who have walked your path.

Ultimately, what you'll gain from this book is more than a guide or a strategy—it's a sense of confidence, a renewed hope, and a belief in your ability to help your child thrive.

As you read through the pages of this book and start implementing the 5-step strategy, you'll begin to notice a shift. A transformation that goes beyond daily routines and spills over into your life in the most beautiful ways.

Picture this: you wake up each morning, not with a sense of dread or fear, but with a renewed confidence in your ability to navigate the day with your child. You look forward to engaging with your little one, armed with the knowledge and strategies to make your interaction productive and enjoyable.

You understand your child's unique ways of communicating, and instead of feeling helpless, you feel empowered.

You see the world through their eyes, appreciating their unique perspective and celebrating their small victories. You find joy in the seemingly simple moments, like sharing a smile or a favorite activity together.

Those sleepless nights spent worrying about the future? They become fewer and farther between. You start to feel a sense of calm and control as you lay out plans for your child's growth and development. You know that challenges will come, but you also know that you're equipped to handle them. The dread of the unknown is replaced by the assurance of knowledge and a solid strategy.

Fast forward a few years, and you will see your child flourishing in their unique way. They are communicating better, engaging more, and even making friends. The best part? You played an integral role in shaping this success.

This is not just an ideal scenario - it is a reality that this book can help you to create. Your journey with your child will be one of learning, growth, and profound connection. It may not always be easy, but it will undoubtedly be rewarding with the right tools and approach.

1

GETTING AN AUTISM DIAGNOSIS

As we begin this journey together, I want to share a fact that initially shocked me but ultimately motivated me towards a deeper understanding and a proactive approach. According to researchers from the Centers for Disease Control and Prevention (CDC), autism rates have risen significantly over the past few decades, even tripling in states like New York and New Jersey. But what does this imply? Is autism spreading rampantly, or are we becoming more conscious of its existence? While the scientific community continues to investigate its exact cause, delving into the roots of autism can offer us invaluable insights and perhaps even illuminate potential pathways to solutions.

In this first chapter, we'll demystify the concept of the autism spectrum and trace its history as a focus of medical study. We'll discuss how the perception and understanding of autism have evolved over time, allowing us to contextualize the current, widely accepted understanding of autism as a spectrum that encapsulates a broad array of conditions.

Our understanding of autism has come a long way since it first entered the domain of medical study. Autism, as a distinct diagnosis, first appeared in the annals of scientific literature in the 1940s through the work of two pioneering researchers: Leo Kanner and Hans Asperger. Although they worked independently and across the Atlantic from each other, both identified and documented children who exhibited a unique set of behavioral traits that didn't align with any known conditions at the time. These traits, characterized by significant challenges in social interactions and non-standard patterns of behavior and interests, laid the foundation for what we understand as autism today.

In his 1943 paper, Kanner, a psychiatrist at Johns Hopkins University, detailed the cases of eleven children he'd observed. He noted their seeming self-absorption, desire for aloneness, and struggle with adapting to change. Around the same time, in Vienna, Asperger was noticing a similar group of children. Unlike Kanner's subjects, the Asperger's group showed less severe social and communicative challenges but displayed rigid routines and a passionate interest in a particular topic. Asperger's observations led to the term "Asperger's Syndrome," a condition often described as a form of "high-functioning" autism.

It wasn't until the latter part of the 20th century that autism began to be considered a spectrum of disorders, encompassing a broad range of conditions. This understanding evolved from the realization that the symptoms and severity of autism vary widely among individuals. This shift in understanding has led to the current diagnosis of Autism Spectrum Disorder (ASD), which recognizes the diversity and individuality of each person with autism.

Today, we appreciate autism as a complex neurodevelopmental disorder that affects people in unique ways, ranging from those who are unable to speak or care for themselves to those who are high-functioning but may struggle with social interaction or have specialized interests. This rich history, along with the ongoing study of autism, has shaped our understanding and management of ASD. Yet, despite the progress made, there is still much to learn and discover in our quest to improve the lives of those with autism.

One of the most crucial points to understand about autism is that it's not a single condition with a one-size-fits-all set of symptoms. Instead, it's a spectrum—a rainbow of experiences and manifestations that can vary incredibly from one person to another. This is what we mean when we refer to Autism Spectrum Disorder or ASD.

The concept of a "spectrum" helps convey that autism can present itself in many different ways and can present with varying degrees of severity. Some individuals may have mild impairments in social interaction but advanced verbal skills and a high IQ. Others may be nonverbal and require significant support to navigate their day-to-day lives. Still, others may fall somewhere in the middle, facing challenges with things like sensory processing or repetitive behaviors but can function independently in other areas.

ASD encompasses conditions previously recognized as separate disorders, such as autism, Asperger's disorder, childhood disintegrative disorder, and pervasive developmental disorder not otherwise specified. This amalgamation reflects the understanding that while these conditions share key features related to social interaction, communication challenges, and repetitive behaviors, they are not separate conditions but rather different expressions along a continuum.

The spectrum nature of autism underscores the need for individualized assessment and intervention. No two people with autism are alike, each presenting a unique set of strengths, challenges, preferences, and ways of understanding the world. Hence, recognizing autism as a spectrum is crucial in shaping our approach to support, education, and intervention - ensuring it is as diverse and multifaceted as individuals.

THE SILVER LINING OF EARLY DIAGNOSIS

While autism is a lifelong condition, decades of research have illuminated one particularly hopeful truth: early intervention can significantly enhance the abilities and improve the life trajectory of children with autism.

The theory of neuroplasticity underpins this crucial finding. Neuroplasticity refers to the brain's ability to reorganize itself by forming new neural connections throughout life. It is most active during early childhood, when the brain is like a sponge, rapidly absorbing information from the environment and adapting in response. In reference to autism, neuroplasticity means that young brains have an exceptional capacity for learning and adapting, offering a window of opportunity to intervene and positively shape a child's development.

Several studies corroborate the transformative potential of early intervention. One of the landmark studies conducted by the University of Washington found that early intervention for toddlers with autism, ages 18 to 30 months, made significant improvements in their IQ, language ability, and social interaction. Another study published in the journal "Pediatrics" found that children who started therapy before age 2.5 years showed more significant improvements than those who began treatment later.

These interventions can vary, from intensive behavior therapy and specialized teaching methods, to speech and occupational therapies. The common thread among these interventions is that they are highly structured, engage the child actively, and are tailored to address the child's individual needs.

However, the key to remember is that "early" does not mean "easier." Parents and caregivers often face overwhelming amounts of information and choices regarding interventions. These decisions can be challenging, but the coming chapters will help you understand these interventions and implement practical strategies that fit your child's needs and your family's situation.

Early intervention doesn't promise a cure—it's important to dispel that notion. However, it provides the tools and strategies to help a child with autism enhance their skills, reduce the impact of symptoms, and maximize their potential. It's about harnessing their abilities, respecting their uniqueness, and setting them up for the best possible future.

NEUROPLASTICITY

Neuroplasticity is a fundamental principle of neuroscience, describing the brain's extraordinary ability to change and adapt over time. From birth and throughout our lives, the brain constantly rewires, reshapes, and refines its countless neural pathways in response to our experiences and interactions with the world around us.

This adaptability is most potent during the early years of life, a period of rapid development and learning known as the critical period. During this time, the brain is exceptionally receptive to environmental stimuli, laying down the foundational architecture for cognitive functions, language acquisition, social skills, and more. This principle enables children to pick up multiple languages with ease or recover from brain injuries more readily than adults.

In the context of autism, neuroplasticity plays a crucial role. Autism is a developmental disorder primarily affecting the brain's structure and function. The power of neuroplasticity provides an opportunity to reshape and redirect these developmental pathways early on. By providing the right stimuli—through early interventions like speech therapy, occupational therapy, and behavioral interventions—we can encourage the brain to form new, healthier connections, fostering skills and behaviors that might otherwise be challenging for a child with autism.

For instance, if a child with autism struggles with social interaction—a common challenge in ASD—early intervention programs could focus on activities that foster social skills, like joint attention, play skills, or understanding emotions. With regular and targeted practice, the child's brain starts forming new neural pathways associated with these skills, leading to improvements in social behavior.

It's important to note that the process is gradual and requires consistency. Neuroplasticity isn't a quick fix but a slow, steady process of reshaping the brain's function. But with early and ongoing intervention, the changes fueled by neuroplasticity can make a significant difference in the lives of children with autism, helping them achieve their fullest potential.

MAKING USE OF THESE STUDIES FROM A PRACTICAL STANDPOINT

While scientific discoveries about autism and neuroplasticity present promising opportunities for positive change, parents often face the challenge of translating these complex studies into practical actions. It's like trying to read a foreign language: you know there's valuable information there, but it's challenging to understand without a proper translation.

For one, scientific studies are typically written for other scientists, using jargon and terminology that might be unfamiliar to the average reader. Additionally, these studies often focus on the 'big picture' findings, discussing outcomes at a high level rather than detailing specific methods or strategies that you could use at home.

Another hurdle lies in the individual nature of autism itself. Autism is a spectrum disorder, meaning it manifests differently in every child. What works for one child may not necessarily work for another. Therefore, parents may need help to discern which strategies or approaches are most likely to be effective for their unique child.

Furthermore, the sheer volume of information available can be overwhelming. With new research being published frequently, keeping up with the latest findings can feel like trying to drink from a firehose. Parents may spend countless hours sifting through dense research papers, trying to determine which ones are credible and relevant.

Finally, even when parents identify potential strategies or treatments, implementing them can be daunting. Many interventions require significant time commitment, professional guidance, or resources that may be limited. And, of course, there's the emotional strain of wanting to do the best for your child but not always knowing how to navigate the complexities of autism.

In essence, while the wealth of autism research provides hope, it also presents a maze of information that parents must navigate. The following chapters aim to simplify this journey, providing practical, actionable tips and strategies based on the latest research findings.

These chapters distill years of scientific research and hands-on experience into a user-friendly guide, focusing not just on explaining the 'what' and 'why' of autism but, most importantly, the 'how.' We delve into specific techniques, interventions, and approaches that have been effective in scientific studies and real-world scenarios, breaking them down into easy-to-follow steps.

Furthermore, the information in these chapters is designed to empower you. We recognize that every child with autism is unique, so we aim to provide a range of strategies you can tailor to suit your child's needs and strengths. You'll be equipped with the tools and knowledge to make informed decisions about your child's care.

Ultimately, this book is about more than just understanding autism. It's about leveraging the latest research findings to enhance your child's abilities, promote their wellbeing, and build a strong, loving connection. In the coming chapters, we will embark on this journey together, navigating the world of autism with actionable tips and strategies. Whether you're a newcomer to this field or have been navigating it for a while, these chapters will provide valuable insights you can apply immediately to your unique situation.

In this opening chapter, we've journeyed through the history of autism, from its inception as a recognized condition to our modern understanding of it as a spectrum of diverse experiences. We've delved into the neuroscience that underpins autism and we have discussed the importance of early intervention, particularly how it can leverage the brain's remarkable neuroplasticity to improve outcomes for children with autism significantly.

We've also identified the difficulties you, as parents, may face in translating academic research into practical, meaningful interventions for your child. However, the understanding and context in this chapter serve as a foundation upon which we will build fundamental, actionable strategies in the coming sections.

As we transition into the next chapter, 'A Mother's Approach to Making the Connection with Your Child,' we will move from the general to the specific. Here, we will focus on how one mother, armed with the knowledge and determination to help her child with autism, created and employed practical strategies to make a meaningful connection with her child. Her experiences, insights, and the wisdom she's accumulated will serve as a roadmap for parents navigating similar journeys. It is an inspiring testament to parental love and a practical guide that will illuminate your path as you embark on this journey with your child.

2

A MOTHER'S APPROACH TO MAKING THE CONNECTION WITH YOUR CHILD

Imagine for a moment you are the conductor of a grand orchestra. Each musician's unique instrument is vital in creating the mesmerizing symphony that resonates in the grand hall. Now, consider your child as the music, the melodious symphony waiting to be orchestrated. As parents, we stand at the helm, our baton poised, shaping the melody, harmonizing the rhythm, and tuning our hearts to the unique resonance of our child's existence. Our role is pivotal, but how do we ensure everyone's in sync? How do we guide the orchestra to create a masterpiece? The answer lies in building a connection with our children and tuning into their unique rhythm and needs. Just like a symphony, parenting children with autism involves understanding their unique tempo and resonance, and that is what this chapter aims to explore.

THE IMPORTANCE OF CONNECTION

Nurturing a deep connection and bonding with your child forms the bedrock of effective parenting. This bond is not just emotional; it's grounded in science and has far-reaching implications on the child's development.

Research shows that parent-child bonding can profoundly affect a child's long-term mental and emotional health. A secure bond promotes self-confidence, boosts emotional and social skills, enhances the child's ability to maintain relationships, and even improves learning outcomes. According to a study published in the National Library of Medicine, children who share a strong emotional bond with their parents show better resilience against stress, anxiety, and depression.

The connection goes beyond the realms of emotional health. It also plays a crucial role in shaping the child's brain. The child's brain is extremely pliable during the early years, growing and changing in response to experiences. The quality of a parent-child relationship greatly influences these experiences, thus directly affecting the brain's development. The consistent, loving interaction between the parent and the child contributes to healthy neural pathways, which form the foundation for future emotional, social, and cognitive behaviors.

Bonding is a dynamic, interactive process that evolves over time. It involves understanding your child's needs, responding to their cues, and creating an environment of trust, security, and mutual respect. This bond becomes the child's first template for interacting with the world. It guides their expectations from relationships, their responses to stress, their ability to manage emotions, and their overall approach to life.

Parenting children with autism intensifies the importance of this bond, given their unique needs and abilities. The bond becomes a secure base from which they navigate their world. Despite the challenges, the power of connection, understanding, and love can pave the way for incredible progress.

WHY THIS IS DOUBLY IMPORTANT WHEN RAISING A CHILD WITH AUTISM

When raising a child with autism, the significance of building a robust and nurturing bond takes on an even deeper meaning. The unique attributes of autism, such as differences in social communication, behavior, and sensory processing, often lead to a distinct set of challenges and experiences for both the child and the parents. Here's why fostering a solid parent-child bond becomes doubly essential in such scenarios:

Enhances Communication: Children with autism often struggle with verbal and non-verbal communication, making it challenging to express their needs or emotions effectively. A close parent-child bond can enhance communication by promoting a deeper understanding of the child's unique ways of expressing themselves.

Supports Social Development: The strong bond and understanding between a parent and an autistic child can form the basis for improving their social interaction skills. Parents can model appropriate social behavior, helping the child to understand and navigate social situations better.

Promotes Emotional Regulation: Many children with autism can experience difficulty managing their emotions, leading to anxiety, meltdowns, or behavioral challenges. A secure bond with parents can provide them with a safe space to navigate their feelings, learn coping strategies, and promote emotional regulation.

Fosters a Sense of Security: Due to their heightened sensory sensitivities and difficulty in adapting to changes, children with autism can often feel overwhelmed by their surroundings. A consistent and understanding parent provides the child with a sense of security and predictability in an otherwise confusing world.

Encourages Learning: The trusting relationship built through a strong connection can also encourage the child to engage in learning activities. It can help parents to introduce and reinforce various skills in a loving and supportive environment.

Improves Quality of Life: A strong parent-child bond can significantly enhance the quality of life for both the child and the parents. It promotes mutual understanding, acceptance, and a loving atmosphere that nurtures the child's growth and development.

Therefore, while fostering a strong connection is integral to all parenting, when raising a child with autism, this bond is more than just essential; it's transformative. This is why the upcoming chapters of this book will focus on providing you with practical strategies and tools to strengthen your bond with your child, enhance their skills, and pave the path to their holistic development.

IT IS DIFFICULT FOR CHILDREN WITH AUTISM TO SIGNAL RECIPROCITY

In typical social interactions, reciprocity - the mutual exchange of communication, emotions, or actions - is crucial. It makes a conversation flow smoothly, a game enjoyable, or a shared experience meaningful. However, children with autism often struggle to signal or engage in reciprocal interactions.

Difficulties in social communication and interaction characterize autism, and this often includes challenges in understanding and responding to the social give-and-take. Here are some ways this might manifest:

Non-Verbal Reciprocity: This could be in the form of eye contact, facial expressions, body language, or gestures. For instance, a child with autism might not make eye contact when spoken to, might not return a smile, or might not use gestures to communicate their needs or desires.

Conversational Reciprocity: In a typical conversation, there's a back-and-forth exchange - one person speaks, the other listens and responds, and so forth. A child with autism might not naturally engage in this kind of conversational turn-taking. They might monopolize a conversation by talking extensively about a favorite topic without checking whether the listener is interested or attempting to involve them with questions or opportunities to respond.

Emotional Reciprocity: This involves sharing emotions with others and responding appropriately to other people's emotions. A child with autism might have difficulty understanding or sharing in another person's feelings. For example, they might not seem comforted by another's attempts to soothe them when they're upset, or they might not show excitement when another person is visibly excited.

Reciprocity in Play: Play activities often involve a give-and-take, such as rolling a ball back and forth or taking turns in a game. A child with autism might prefer solitary play activities and may not naturally engage in shared, reciprocal play.

These challenges can often make it difficult for children with autism to form and maintain relationships, leading to frustration or isolation. However, it's important to remember that while children with autism may communicate or interact differently, they can still form meaningful connections with others. Through strategies tailored to their unique needs and strengths - as we will explore in the subsequent chapters - we can facilitate and encourage reciprocity in their interactions.

KIDS WITH AUTISM GENERALLY NEED MORE SUPERVISION

Children with autism spectrum disorder (ASD) tend to require more supervision than their neurotypical peers. This is due to various factors related to the nature of autism, which may include social communication challenges, sensory sensitivities, repetitive behaviors, and a need for routine and predictability. Here's a closer look at why more supervision is generally necessary:

Safety Concerns: Kids with autism often have difficulty recognizing danger or understanding safety rules. They might not comprehend why running into a street, touching a hot stove, or approaching an unfamiliar dog, for instance, is unsafe. This lack of instinctive self-preservation necessitates a higher degree of supervision to ensure their safety.

Social Challenges: The social world can be confusing and overwhelming for a child with autism. They may struggle with interpreting social cues, understanding others' perspectives, or managing social interactions. Close supervision can help guide them through these complex social situations and help them navigate social norms more effectively.

Sensory Sensitivities: Children with autism often have unique sensory needs or sensitivities. They may be hypersensitive to certain sounds, textures, tastes, or smells and react strongly to sensory experiences that seem mundane to others. As such, they may require more supervision to ensure their environment is not causing them undue stress or discomfort.

Difficulty with Transitions: Changes in routine or unexpected transitions can be particularly challenging for children with autism, leading to distress or difficult behaviors. Close supervision allows parents or caregivers to anticipate and manage these transitions, minimizing potential stress and ensuring a smooth changeover from one activity to another.

Repetitive Behaviors: Kids with autism often engage in repetitive behaviors, ranging from harmless routines or rituals to potentially harmful self-stimulatory behaviors. More supervision can help manage these behaviors, redirecting harmful ones and leveraging harmless ones to facilitate learning or comfort.

Wandering or Elopement: Many children with autism tend to wander or elope from safe environments, often driven by curiosity, a desire to escape an overwhelming situation or a pull towards specific interests or attractions. This can pose significant safety risks, making constant supervision essential.

It's important to note that every child with autism is unique, and their need for supervision will depend on their individual characteristics, abilities, and challenges. While they may require more care, they also possess unique strengths and potential that can be nurtured and developed with the right support and strategies to help them lead fulfilling lives.

RECENT DEVELOPMENTS IN AUTISM RESEARCH

Recent years have brought some fascinating developments in autism research that have significantly advanced our understanding of this complex condition. Here are a few of these scientific insights and discoveries that have shifted the way medical researchers and professionals approach autism:

Genetics: Autism has a strong genetic basis. While no single gene is identified as the cause of autism, researchers have identified over 100 genes associated with increased risk for autism. Many of these genes are involved in brain development or communication between brain cells (neurons). It's also important to note that genetic factors can interact with environmental influences, suggesting that both nature and nurture play a role in autism.

Neurological Factors: Autism has been associated with differences in brain structure and function. For example, studies using brain imaging techniques have shown differences in the size and connectivity of specific brain regions in individuals with autism. However, these differences are not consistent across all individuals with autism, reflecting the diversity of this condition.

The Gut-Brain Axis: A growing body of evidence shows a connection between the gut and the brain, known as the gut-brain axis. Many individuals with autism have gastrointestinal issues, and research suggests that the gut microbiome (the community of microorganisms living in our intestines) could influence brain development and behavior. Some studies have even found that certain probiotics can improve symptoms of autism, although this is still a relatively new and rapidly evolving field of research.

Early Detection and Diagnosis: The earlier we can identify autism, the earlier intervention strategies can start, which is associated with better outcomes. Researchers have made strides in identifying early behavioral signs of autism, allowing for diagnosis in toddlers or even babies. There's also emerging research exploring biological markers of autism (such as differences in brain imaging or genetic markers), which could enable even earlier detection.

Personalized Approaches: Given the diversity of autism (hence the term "autism spectrum"), there's growing recognition that a one-size-fits-all approach is ineffective. Instead, personalized treatment strategies that consider the individual's unique strengths, challenges, interests, and needs are ideal. This is supported by research into subtypes of autism and the factors that contribute to individual differences in symptoms and outcomes.

Importance of Early Intervention: Research continues to emphasize the significance of early intervention in autism. With various therapeutic approaches, the goal is to capitalize on the young brain's plasticity to improve outcomes. Interventions focusing on building social communication skills, promoting engagement and interaction, and reducing challenging behaviors are particularly effective.

Each of these insights and discoveries has shifted the understanding and approach to autism, paving the way for more effective diagnosis, intervention, and support strategies. It is a testament to the ongoing commitment of the scientific and medical communities to enhance the lives of individuals with autism and their families.

It's an exciting time in autism research, with these advancements offering new hope and possibilities for individuals with autism and their families. It's important to remember that our understanding of autism continues to evolve, and future research will undoubtedly shed more light on this complex condition.

THE JASPER MODEL AND ITS FOCUS

Joint Attention, Symbolic Play, Engagement and Regulation (JASPER): JASPER is an evidence-based treatment strategy for young children with autism. Developed by researchers at UCLA, it aims to boost children's social and communication skills by enhancing their ability to engage, attend, and play. This model uses naturalistic behavioral strategies, employing the child's interests and natural settings to motivate engagement and learning. It's main aspects include:

Joint Attention: Joint attention refers to the shared focus of two individuals on an object or event. It is crucial for social development and communication, as it involves understanding that someone else has a focus of attention, and one can share that focus. In the context of autism, children often have difficulty with joint attention. JASPER uses specific strategies to build these skills, such as following the child's lead, using child-directed language, and creating opportunities for the child to initiate joint attention.

Play: Symbolic play is a type of play that involves using objects or actions to represent other objects or actions. It's essential for cognitive and language development. In JASPER, play is used to encourage joint attention, engagement, and social communication. Therapists or parents are encouraged to join in the child's play, expand on it, and create opportunities for interaction and communication.

Engagement: Engagement, or the child's active involvement and interest in activities, is a crucial part of JASPER. Strategies to promote engagement include using highly preferred toys and activities, reducing distractions, and taking turns during play. Increased engagement is associated with better learning outcomes.

Communication: JASPER aims to improve both verbal and non-verbal communication. This includes initiating communication, maintaining interactions, and taking turns. Techniques like using simple language, waiting for the child to respond, and modeling correct responses are used.

Mirrored Pacing and Imitation: This refers to matching the child's pace during interactions. By attuning to the child's tempo and style of play, the adult can foster a more meaningful connection, reduce frustration, and encourage the child's active participation.

In summary, JASPER is a comprehensive and individualized approach that harnesses a child's interests and natural settings to improve their social communication skills. Focusing on joint attention, play, engagement, communication, and mirrored pacing offers a practical framework for enhancing the connection between parents and their children with autism.

This book takes its inspiration directly from the proven concepts of the JASPER model, a well-researched and practical approach to enhancing the social and communication skills of children with autism. The techniques and strategies presented here are designed to make it easier for parents to forge a robust and meaningful connection with their children.

However, this book goes beyond merely explaining the JASPER model. It bridges the gap between scientific research and the everyday reality of parenting a child with autism. It aims to demystify the principles of JASPER and break them down into practical, easy-to-implement steps that you can seamlessly incorporate into daily routines and interactions.

Moreover, this book also integrates additional tips and insights from real-life experiences of parents navigating the journey of raising a child with autism. These insights provide valuable perspective, making the strategies more relatable, understandable, and feasible.

This book offers parents a comprehensive guide - a fusion of scientifically-backed strategies from the JASPER model and practical wisdom from parents who've walked the same path. It's designed to equip you with the knowledge and tools to build a solid, fulfilling connection with your child, fostering their development and enriching your shared experience.

A BREAKDOWN OF THE FIVE CORE COMPONENTS OF OUR APPROACH

The methods outlined in this book are built around five core components, each closely related to the principles of the JASPER model. These components are designed to be accessible, practical, and beneficial to both parent and child in their journey together. These fundamental concepts include:

Stay Front and Center: This component emphasizes the importance of a parent's physical presence in their child's space. It's about actively participating in your child's activities, not just supervising from the sidelines. Engage with them in play, initiate activities that you both can enjoy, and aim to be a part of their world. This constant interaction helps to establish a strong bond and lays the groundwork for effective communication. By positioning yourself front and center, you become an integral part of your child's world, fostering an environment that encourages social and communication development.

Teaching Gestures: Non-verbal communication plays a crucial role in the interaction process. Teaching your child gestures for different needs and emotions can aid in expressing their feelings and thoughts. It can serve as a bridge to developing speech and language skills.

Following Their Lead and Teaching Imitation: This aspect emphasizes the importance of entering your child's world. It means imitating their actions, showing interest in their activities, and building on what they are already engaged in. This approach makes interactions more enjoyable for the child and encourages social connection and communication. The act of mirroring or imitating your child's activities and playing at their pace builds engagement and teaches the social aspect of learning through imitation.

Creating Joint Interactions: This component is about fostering 'joint attention'. It involves engaging your child's attention on a shared object or activity, which aids in creating an interactive communication environment. It's about reciprocating and building on your child's interests and actions. It forms the basis for further social-communication growth.

Teaching Receptive and Expressive Language: All children with autism have different ways they communicate. Using simple approaches, we can improve and strengthen their skills with both receptive and expressive language to build a strong social connection and increase interaction.

Each of these components is interconnected and mutually reinforcing. When applied consistently and patiently, they can foster a stronger connection between you and your child, significantly improving their social and communication skills. This book will also give many examples of how to use these approaches in your daily routines. This makes them a simple and straightforward way to add them into activities you already are doing. Daily routines offer familiar and structured settings that can be excellent opportunities for interaction. This book will help identify these opportunities in routine activities like mealtime, bath time, or bedtime and use them to engage your child. This approach can make learning more natural and integrated into your child's daily life.

In this chapter, we explored the profound importance of forging a deep connection with your child, particularly for those living with Autism Spectrum Disorder (ASD). By delving into scientific research, we discovered many ways that being closely connected positively impacts your child's development and well-being. We also discussed how the unique challenges associated with ASD, such as the difficulty in signaling reciprocity and the need for greater supervision, make establishing this connection even more critical.

We journeyed through the most recent advances in autism research, taking a closer look at the strides made in genetic studies, neurological discoveries, and the fascinating connection to the gut microbiome. We also touched on the increasingly early diagnosis of autism, offering hope for the early intervention that proves so beneficial.

The highlight of the chapter was undoubtedly the introduction of the JASPER model, a widely recognized and science-backed approach for assisting children with autism. We discussed how the JASPER model's elements form the foundation for important development skills for young kids with autism.

As we move into the following chapters, we will be discussing the five core components of this book's approach:

- Staying front and center
- Teaching gestures and nonverbal communication
- Following your child's lead and teaching imitation
- Creating joint interactions
- Building receptive and expressive communication

In chapter 3, we will delve deeper into the first core component of our approach. Here, we'll explore practical strategies and techniques to help you become the conductor of your child's unique orchestra, tuning into their needs and creating a harmony that benefits both of your lives.

3

BUILDING ENGAGEMENT: BEING FRONT AND CENTER

Building a connection with a child who has autism can often feel like trying to decipher an intricate code. These children can struggle with relating to others and tend to withdraw into their own world, leading parents to feel like they're navigating a one-way street. However, it's important to note that this does not reflect a lack of desire to connect but is instead indicative of the unique ways children with autism engage with and perceive their surroundings. One of the early challenges parents commonly face is figuring out how to bridge this gap effectively and initiate engagement with their children. This chapter will guide you through understanding and implementing strategies that help to form this crucial connection, emphasizing the concept of 'being front and center' in your child's world.

Children with Autism Spectrum Disorder (ASD) often face significant social interaction and communication challenges. They tend to perceive, interpret, and respond to social cues differently from neurotypical individuals, and these differences can make it difficult for them to connect with others in conventional ways.

There are a few reasons why this is the case. Firstly, many children with autism have difficulty with theory of mind, or understanding that other people have thoughts, feelings, and perspectives different from their own. This can make it hard for them to predict or understand others' reactions, making social interactions confusing and stressful.

Secondly, they often have difficulty reading and interpreting non-verbal cues such as facial expressions, body language, and tone of voice. Given that much of human communication is non-verbal, this can be a significant barrier to successful social interactions. For example, a child with autism might not understand that a frown indicates unhappiness or that a specific tone of voice conveys sarcasm.

Moreover, many children with autism are hyper- or hyposensitive to sensory stimuli. They might find certain noises, lights, or touch sensations overwhelming or distressing, further complicating social interactions. For example, the background noise in a crowded room, which most people can filter out, might be unbearably loud and chaotic for a child with autism.

As a result of these challenges, children with autism might withdraw or isolate themselves as a coping mechanism. The world can seem unpredictable and overwhelming to them, and withdrawal can be a way of managing these feelings.

Understanding these challenges can help parents and caregivers empathize with their children better and create strategies to promote meaningful engagement and connection. Despite these challenges, children with autism can form strong, loving relationships with others – they may do so in their unique ways.

Knowing the unique challenges children with autism face in social interactions is the first step toward understanding how to engage with them effectively. Early engagement is particularly crucial in the development of children with autism, as it can significantly influence their ability to connect with others, learn new skills, and navigate their world.

Creating opportunities for interaction, adjusting our communication styles, and adopting a responsive approach can profoundly impact their social and cognitive development. Stanford Children's Health recommends several strategies to foster engagement with children with autism:

Provide a structured environment: Children with autism often thrive in environments where routines are consistent and where they know what to expect. Structured play activities, predictable daily schedules, and visual cues can make the world more understandable for them.

Focus on non-verbal communication: Because children with autism often struggle with verbal communication, non-verbal forms of interaction can be very effective. This can involve using gestures, facial expressions, visual aids, or physical prompts to communicate.

Use their interests to motivate engagement: Every child has unique interests, which can be used as a stepping stone for interaction. For instance, if a child is fascinated by trains, using train-themed activities can help motivate them to engage.

Break down tasks into manageable steps: This can help make activities more understandable and less overwhelming for children with autism. For example, instead of instructing a child to clean their room, you might break the task down into individual steps like picking up toys, making the bed, etc.

Adopt a playful approach: Play can be an excellent way to engage children with autism. It allows them to explore, experiment, and learn in a relaxed and enjoyable setting.

In light of the difficulties that children with autism often face in making sense of social interactions, developing strategies for early engagement is not only beneficial, but necessary. The next section of this chapter will delve deeper into practical methods of fostering engagement and interaction.

THE KEY TO BUILDING ENGAGEMENT

Staying "front and center" in your child's visual field is a crucial strategy for engaging with a child on the autism spectrum. Children with autism are predominantly visual learners, meaning they comprehend and interact with the world most effectively through what they see. Being in front of your child helps ensure they pay attention to you and provides opportunities for interaction and communication.

There are several key reasons why being front and center is essential:

Grabs Attention: The first step to engagement is grabbing your child's attention. When you position yourself directly in their line of sight, you naturally become a point of focus.

Facilitates Non-Verbal Communication: Much of our communication is non-verbal, including facial expressions, gestures, and body language. Being in front of your child allows them to observe these non-verbal cues more efficiently, which can support their understanding and learning.

Supports Joint Attention: Joint attention refers to the shared focus of two individuals on an object, facilitated by eye-gazing, pointing, or other verbal or non-verbal indications. This critical social communication skill is often challenging for children with autism. You can more effectively engage your child in joint attention activities by being front and center.

Promotes Interaction: When you are physically at your child's level and within their field of vision, it encourages them to interact with you. This could be through eye contact, mimicking actions, or responding to your cues.

Remember, the key is not just about being physically present but also being actively engaging and responsive. This might mean singing a song, playing a game, or involving your child in a task. The goal is to create an environment where your child feels encouraged to interact and communicate. In the following sections, we'll explore specific strategies and activities to help you implement this concept.

Visual learning is often a strong suit for many people with Autism Spectrum Disorder (ASD). This is partly due to the unique ways in which their brains process information. Here's how this preference for visual learning manifests and why it's important:

Visual Thinking: Many individuals with autism are strong visual thinkers. They might think in pictures or visual patterns rather than in words. Dr. Temple Grandin, a well-known autism advocate and herself an individual with autism, has described her own thinking as "thinking in pictures," much like a series of video clips in her mind.

Concrete and Literal Interpretation: People with ASD often interpret information more concretely and literally than their neurotypical peers. Visual aids, such as pictures, diagrams, and charts, can provide clear, concise, and concrete information that aligns well with this thinking style.

Visual Memory Strengths: Many individuals with ASD have excellent visual memory. They can remember and recall visual information, like images or places, far better than verbal or auditory information. This can make visual aids a very effective tool for teaching and learning.

Helps Manage Change: Visual schedules and aids can help people with ASD manage changes in routine, transition between activities, or understand what is expected of them, reducing anxiety and confusion.

Supports Communication and Social Interaction: Visual supports like PECS (Picture Exchange Communication System), social stories, or visual cue cards can aid communication, expressing emotions, and understanding social expectations.

For these reasons, using visual strategies such as visual aids, visual schedules, and other forms of visual stimuli are often central to educational programs and therapeutic approaches for individuals with ASD. Being "front and center," or within the direct line of sight of your child, allows you to leverage these visual strengths, helping your child to better understand and interact with their environment.

STAY FRONT AND CENTER IN PRACTICE

Staying "front and center" is a key strategy in engaging children with autism and maintaining their attention and connection. Given the inherent visual strengths and preferences of many individuals with autism, this positioning allows parents to capitalize on those strengths.

Here's how being front and center works in practical terms:

Visual Engagement: Being directly in your child's line of sight makes it easier for them to focus on you. Your facial expressions, gestures, and actions become more noticeable and easier to interpret.

Improved Communication: Communication is more than just verbal language. It's about facial expressions, body language, and tone of voice. When you're front and center, your child can pick up on these nonverbal cues better.

Joint Attention: Staying front and center helps facilitate joint attention, which is critical for language development and social interaction. This involves the shared focus of two individuals on an object or activity, facilitated by eye contact, pointing, or other verbal or non-verbal indications.

Modeling Behavior: Being in the direct line of sight makes it easier for your child to observe and learn from your actions. This is particularly beneficial for teaching new skills or behaviors.

Building Connection: The consistent presence in your child's direct visual field can foster a stronger bond. It sends a message of being available, interested, and engaged in what they are doing.

However, it's also important to remember to give children with autism some space and respect their comfort levels. Staying front and center is about being accessible and present rather than intrusive. Therefore, it's crucial to observe and respond to your child's signals about their feelings and whether they need some alone time.

Building a strong connection with a child with autism involves more than being physically present and attentive. Understanding their world and engaging with them on their terms requires a conscious effort. Here are some additional tips that might help:

Join their world: Children with autism often engage in repetitive activities or fixate on specific topics. Instead of trying to shift their focus, join them in their interests. This can help build rapport and provide a foundation for expanding their interests over time.

Use their interests to motivate learning: If your child is particularly interested in trains, for example, you can use trains to teach counting, colors, or reading. This makes learning more interesting and relevant for them.

Follow their lead: Let your child lead during play or other activities. This gives them a sense of control and makes the interaction more enjoyable. It can also provide valuable insights into their preferences and abilities.

Communicate at their level: Use simple, clear language and visual aids to communicate with your child. If they use non-verbal cues or express themselves uniquely, try to incorporate these into your own communication.

Create a predictable environment: Children with autism often feel more comfortable in structured, predictable environments. Regular routines and clear rules can help them feel more secure and reduce anxiety.

Encourage social interaction: Find ways to gently encourage social interaction, whether it's with family members, other children, or even pets. This can help them develop social skills in a safe, comfortable environment.

Celebrate their strengths: Every child has unique strengths and abilities. Celebrating these can boost their confidence and provide opportunities for connection. This could be as simple as praising them for a job well done or taking an active interest in their hobbies.

Remember that every child with autism is unique, and what works for one may not work for another. Getting to know your child and adapting these strategies to suit their needs and preferences is essential.

BUILDING A BRIDGE

"Building a bridge" is a metaphor often used in autism intervention to describe joining your child in their world to foster a strong connection. This approach emphasizes the importance of understanding, appreciating, and engaging with your child's unique interests, behaviors, and ways of interacting.

Here's how this can be done:

Observation: Observe your child's play patterns, interests, and behaviors. This will help you understand their preferences and how they interact with the world around them.

Joining in Their Interests: Once you understand what they enjoy, engage in those activities with them. If your child enjoys lining up toy cars, sit down and join them in this activity. It's not about steering them toward a different action but meeting them where they are.

Non-Directive Play: Let your child lead the play. This is known as "child-directed play." It helps to build rapport, trust, and engagement. It also allows your child to feel a sense of control and can reduce anxiety.

Imitation: Imitate your child's behaviors during play. This can validate their interests and help them feel understood. It can also encourage reciprocal interaction and turn-taking.

Expanding Play: Once you've joined your child in their world and established a strong connection, you can gently expand their play. For instance, if your child is lining up cars, you might introduce a new element, like a toy garage or a bridge, to add a new dimension to their play.

This "bridge" you're building serves as a conduit for communication and learning. It's about meeting your child where they are, fostering a connection based on understanding and acceptance, and then gradually expanding their world in a comfortable and meaningful way. This strategy forms a foundational part of many successful autism interventions and therapies.

THE FIRST STEP TO CREATING BACK-AND-FORTH INTERACTION

Creating a back-and-forth interaction, also known as reciprocal interaction, is a fundamental goal when building a connection with your child who has autism. Reciprocity refers to the natural give-and-take that occurs in social interactions, where one person's behavior influences and is influenced by another person's behavior.

This might seem like an intuitive part of social interaction for many, but for children with autism, reciprocal exchange can be particularly challenging to grasp. This is due to the social-communication difficulties that are central to autism.

Using the "building a bridge" strategy, you take that essential first step toward reciprocal interaction. You're establishing a solid connection with your child on their terms, in their world, which makes them more likely to be open to engagement.

You're showing them how interaction works by joining in on your child's interests and imitating their behaviors. You're modeling the behavior that you want to see from them, which can, in turn, encourage them to start engaging in back-and-forth interaction.

The goal is to gradually move from parallel play, where you and your child are playing side by side but not really interacting, to interactive play, where you're engaged in a shared activity, and there is a back-and-forth exchange.

Remember, this is a process, and progress might be slow. It's important to be patient, persistent, and celebrate every small step your child makes toward reciprocal interaction. The foundation you build here will be crucial for their future social-communication development.

LOOK FOR REPETITIVE BEHAVIORS

Repetitive behaviors, often referred to as "stimming" (short for self-stimulating behaviors), are common in individuals with autism. These behaviors can take various forms, such as hand-flapping, rocking, spinning, lining up toys, or repeating words or phrases.

Repetitive behaviors can serve various functions for a child with autism. They can provide comfort, help the child cope with anxiety or sensory overload, or offer enjoyment. In this context, they can also be an entry point for parents and caregivers to connect with their children.

When you notice these repetitive behaviors, it is crucial to recognize their importance for your child rather than trying to change or stop them. By understanding their function, you can use these behaviors as a bridge to join your child in their world and strengthen your connection.

For instance, if your child likes to line up their toys, instead of discouraging the behavior, join in. Participate in the activity by adding a toy to the line or carefully move one and watch their reaction. This not only validates their interests but also allows you to introduce a shared activity, gradually leading to more interactive play.

It's essential, however, to seek professional advice if repetitive behaviors become harmful or excessively interfere with daily life. Safe alternatives or strategies to manage these behaviors might be necessary in these cases. But in general, embracing your child's unique ways of interacting with the world can be a valuable tool for building your connection.

IDENTIFY YOUR CHILD'S NATURAL MOTIVATION

Identifying your child's natural motivations can play a pivotal role in engagement and connection. Each child with autism, like any child, will have their own unique set of interests, preferences, and inclinations. These motivations can be powerful tools for promoting learning, engagement, and interaction.

Natural motivations could be in the form of specific activities (such as painting or listening to music), objects (such as a favorite toy or book), sensory experiences (like the feeling of sand or the sound of wind chimes), or routines (such as bedtime stories or mealtime rituals).

You can identify these motivations by observing your child closely. What activities do they gravitate towards during their free time? Which objects do they seem most attracted to? What can hold their attention longer than other things? These observations can provide insight into your child's inner world and their natural motivators.

Once you've identified these motivators, you can use them as a springboard for interaction and engagement. For instance, if your child is particularly interested in cars, you might incorporate toy cars into learning activities or use them as a reward for completing tasks.

Importantly, leveraging these natural motivations isn't about manipulation; it's about joining your child in their world and using what they love to foster engagement and interaction. This approach respects your child's unique interests and paves the way for more meaningful connections.

CONNECTING THROUGH PLAY

Play is a vital aspect of child development, and for children with ASD, it takes on an even more crucial role. It provides an engaging context within which children can learn and practice various skills, from communication and social interaction to problem-solving and emotional regulation. When we think of play from the perspective of staying front and center and building a bridge, it becomes a powerful tool to facilitate engagement and connection. Thus, we want to make our first goal of changing our play approach to the following steps:

Staying Front and Center: In the context of play, being front and center means positioning yourself within your child's attentional field, participating in their play activities, and guiding their engagement. This doesn't necessarily mean directing the play but being an active participant and facilitator. Children with ASD often learn best visually, so when you are in their direct line of sight, it becomes easier for them to engage with you, understand your gestures and expressions, and learn from your actions. When you engage in play, ensure you are at your child's eye level, which will help you maintain a visual connection, better read their cues, and respond appropriately.

Building a Bridge: This involves entering your child's world of play, understanding their interests, and making connections based on these interests. If your child loves spinning wheels, for example, instead of trying to redirect them to a different type of play, join them. Spin wheels with them and gradually introduce new elements to expand the play—like making car noises, moving the car around, or setting up a pretend car wash. Doing so builds a bridge between their world and yours, using play as the platform. Through this shared, interactive experience, your child will feel more connected to you and be more open to learning new skills.

Play, in essence, serves as a natural, enjoyable, and effective means of building engagement with your child on the autism spectrum. When we adapt our approach to their unique needs and interests, we create a supportive, positive environment where they can thrive.

PLAY IS ABOUT INTERACTION

At its heart, play is about interaction. It's a natural way for children to communicate, connect, and engage with the world around them. For children, play is a language that expresses their feelings, thoughts, and understanding of their environment.

For children with Autism Spectrum Disorder, interaction through play can sometimes be challenging due to their unique sensory needs or social communication difficulties. However, this doesn't diminish the importance of play; it makes play a crucial avenue for them to practice and improve these skills.

Interactive play offers a safe and comfortable setting for a child to explore different social roles, understand the rules of social behavior, and learn how to engage with others. Through various forms of play, children can develop crucial skills such as turn-taking, sharing, empathizing, and problem-solving.

For children with ASD, guided interactive play can be a potent tool for parents and therapists. The repetitive and structured nature of many play activities can be soothing and accessible for these children, making play an excellent way to encourage interaction. As parents, caregivers, and therapists play with the child, they can gradually introduce new interactive elements, encouraging them to participate more fully and engage with them in increasingly complex ways.

Hence, when we say, "play is about interaction," we recognize its role as a facilitator for children, especially those with ASD, to learn, practice, and understand the complexities of social interaction in a fun and comfortable way.

Different types of play that the reader can use to interact and build a connection with their child

Parents can use several types of play to engage with their children, particularly those with Autism Spectrum Disorder (ASD). Each style of play provides different benefits and opportunities for interaction and connection:

Exploratory Play: This type involves exploring and examining the world around them. It can include playing with different objects, textures, or toys to explore their properties. This kind of play can benefit children with ASD because it allows them to engage in a sensory-rich environment at their own pace.

Symbolic Play: Also known as pretend or imaginative play, symbolic play involves using objects, actions, or ideas to represent other objects, actions, or ideas. It can be more challenging for children with ASD due to difficulties in social imagination. Still, encouragement and guidance can be a valuable way for them to express their thoughts or feelings.

Constructive Play: Constructive play includes any play activity where children create or construct something. This can be building with blocks, drawing, or crafting. This type of play can help improve motor skills, spatial awareness, and planning skills. It can also provide joint attention and cooperative play opportunities if building something together.

Physical Play: Physical or active play includes any activity that gets children moving. For children with ASD, this can be an excellent way to help manage their energy levels and provide sensory input.

Social Play: Social play involves playing games or activities with others. This type of play can be more challenging for children with ASD due to difficulties with social interaction, but it can be a valuable way to build social skills and learn about cooperation and turn-taking.

Routine-based Play: This involves integrating play into daily routines like mealtime, bath time, or bedtime. For children with ASD, who often thrive on routine and predictability, routine-based play can be a comforting and engaging way to interact.

Remember, the key to playing with a child with ASD is to follow their lead, engage in activities they enjoy, and gradually introduce new elements to help them expand their skills and abilities. Using play as a way to interact with your child not only builds connection but also provides a foundation for developing social, communication, and cognitive skills.

EXPLORATORY PLAY

Exploratory play, often known as sensory or discovery play, is a fundamental form of engagement for children, particularly those with Autism Spectrum Disorder (ASD). This type of play is characterized by curiosity, examination, and discovery and allows children to experience the world around them using their senses — touch, sight, sound, smell, and taste.

For a child with ASD, exploratory play is a key way to understand and navigate their environment at their own pace. It encourages curiosity and can often help in sensory regulation, a common challenge for many children with ASD.

For instance, playing with textured toys or materials, like sand, water, play dough, or even different fabrics, can provide various sensory experiences. The child is allowed to explore these textures, understanding their properties and how they react to different actions — for instance, how sand slips through the fingers or how water splashes.

Observing your child first and identifying when they are most approachable or accessible is crucial during exploratory play. This can help you join the play in a way that aligns with your child's interests and current engagement.

Using the child's interests as a foundation, you can gradually introduce new items or ideas for exploration. For example, if your child is fascinated by water, you might introduce different objects that float or sink or add color to the water with safe, non-toxic dyes.

During these play sessions, you should keep instructions or directions short and simple. The focus is on independent exploration and discovery, and too much direction may hinder the child's engagement.

The goal of exploratory play isn't to achieve a particular outcome but rather to provide the child an opportunity to engage, explore, and learn about the world in a way that feels safe and enjoyable to them. And importantly, these moments of play are also an opportunity for parents to connect, build a stronger relationship, and understand their child's unique way of experiencing the world.

USE WHAT YOU HAVE AROUND YOU

Engaging your child with ASD in play doesn't necessarily require specialized toys or equipment. You can use everyday items around you to create engaging and enriching play experiences. Let's break down how you can use these everyday items to encourage play:

Balloons: Balloons can be used creatively to engage a child. For instance, you could inflate a balloon and let it go to watch it fly around, which can help teach your child about cause and effect. Or, you could play a simple game of keeping the balloon in the air using your hands. This can help improve gross motor skills and hand-eye coordination.

Bubbles: Bubbles are a great tool for visual engagement and sensory play. Watching bubbles float in the air and burst can be fascinating for children with ASD. It can be a calming activity and can also be used to encourage children to reach out and pop the bubbles, promoting gross motor skills and eye-hand coordination.

Cause and Effect Toys: Toys like pop-up toys, toy hammers, or simple push-and-go cars can be great for teaching the principle of cause and effect. These toys can also promote fine motor skills and problem-solving abilities.

Blocks: Building blocks can be an excellent tool for developing spatial skills and creativity. They can also be used to encourage interaction, for example, by building a tower together. You can use colorful blocks to teach about different colors and shapes.

Simple Puzzles: Puzzles with large pieces and clear pictures can be an excellent tool for teaching problem-solving skills. You can use them to promote fine motor skills, hand-eye coordination, and shape recognition.

Interactive Books: Interactive books with different textures, pop-up pictures, or sounds can create a rich sensory experience. Reading together can promote language and cognitive skills and provide opportunities for you to connect with your child, especially if you animate the reading with different voices and emotions.

Remember, these activities aim to engage your child, build a connection, and make the play experience enjoyable for both of you. It can pave the way for improved social interaction and communication skills.

SOCIAL GAMES AND SONGS WITH GESTURES

Social games and songs with gestures are highly beneficial tools for children with ASD. They help boost interaction, promote joint attention, and enhance language skills. These activities can also help the child to engage more effectively with the world around them. Let's dive into the specifics of each:

Songs with Gestures: Songs like "Wheels on the Bus," "Itsy Bitsy Spider," and "Patty Cake" can be very engaging for children with ASD. These songs are fun to sing and include accompanying hand motions or gestures. These help the child to connect the movements with the words in the song, thus supporting their language and motor skills development. Additionally, such songs can be a tool to encourage eye contact and joint attention as you can playfully engage with your child while singing and making the movements together.

Chase Games: Games like tag or hide-and-seek can be modified to suit your child's comfort level and ability. Such games encourage social interaction and allow your child to understand concepts like taking turns and following rules. They can also help in developing gross motor skills and spatial awareness.

Swinging Games: Activities that incorporate swinging can be incredibly soothing and beneficial for a child with autism, as they provide a unique sensory experience. This could be as simple as pushing your child on a swing at the park or creating a makeshift swing at home with a blanket. These games can improve balance, coordination, and body awareness.

Be patient and follow your child's lead. They may not get the hang of these activities right away, and that's perfectly fine. The primary goal here is to facilitate engagement and connection, and over time, your child will likely start responding more to these social games and songs.

BEING FRONT AND CENTER THROUGHOUT DAILY ROUTINES

Being front and center during daily routines offers many opportunities to strengthen the bond between you and your child and foster their growth and development. The key is approaching each task as a moment of connection and learning. Here are a few daily routines that can be transformed into meaningful interaction opportunities:

Setting the Table at Meals: Involve your child in setting the table. This can help them understand sequences, recognize various utensils, and contribute to a shared task. You can narrate each action, explaining what you're doing and why, which can also enhance their language skills.

Sitting Together for Meals: Meals offer a great opportunity for interaction. Sit face-to-face with your child so that they can see your expressions as you eat and talk. This can help your child understand social cues, foster communication skills, and develop good eating habits.

Reading a Book: When reading a book, make sure your child can see your face and the book. Point to the book's characters, objects, and actions, and explain them. This can facilitate understanding and promote joint attention.

Getting Dressed: Comment on body parts or clothing items while dressing your child. For example, say, "Here are your socks, let's put them on your feet." This can improve their language skills and their understanding of their own body.

Taking a Bath: Make bath time more enjoyable and engaging by incorporating play into it. Use bath toys to create stories, sing songs, or explain the process of bathing.

Incorporating engagement strategies into daily routines can significantly impact your child's development. It helps turn ordinary moments into teachable opportunities, all while deepening the bond between you and your child. It's important to remember to follow your child's pace and take cues from their interests and comfort levels.

MORE ON BATH TIME

Bath time can often be a challenging routine for children with autism. However, it can become an enjoyable and bonding experience with thoughtful planning and practice.

Help Them Feel Secure: Many children with autism can feel overwhelmed by the sensory experiences during bath time. The feeling of water, the temperature change, the smell of soap, or the sound of running water can be intense. Therefore, it's essential to make them feel secure. This can be achieved by gradually introducing them to the water, starting with a small amount and gradually increasing. Let them bring a comforting object into the bath if that helps. Also, consider using a bath mat to prevent slipping and a towel or inflatable bath pillow for added comfort.

"Heavy Work" Before Bath Time: This refers to sensory input or activities that involve pushing or pulling against the body. This type of activity, often called "heavy work", can be very calming for children with autism. Hugging, for example, provides deep pressure that can be soothing. Thus, a firm hug or carrying your child to the bath can be an effective transitional activity, preparing them for the change in activity and environment.

Incorporate Play into Taking Baths: Turning bath time into play time can make the process more enjoyable for your child. Use waterproof toys your child enjoys, such as rubber ducks, boats, or water-friendly books. You can also use bath crayons for wall doodling or have fun with bubble-making. Remember, the goal is to keep the experience positive, relaxing, and engaging, which will help build connections and make your child more receptive to learning and interaction.

Take it slowly, respect your child's comfort level, and be patient. Over time, with consistent practice and positive experiences, bath time can become an anticipated and enjoyable routine for both of you.

This chapter explored the importance of building solid and meaningful connections with children with autism. This chapter explained that children with autism can struggle to relate to others, causing them to withdraw into themselves. It emphasized the need for parents to understand how to engage with their children from an early stage.

To build engagement, the chapter highlighted the key of being visually accessible or 'front and center' to maintain attention and connection, since children with ASD typically learn best visually. It explored various strategies to foster this connection, from joining the child's world and building a bridge to initiating back-and-forth interactions.

The chapter also delved into the world of play, establishing it as a critical means of interaction. Different types of play, like exploratory play, were discussed, with the suggestion to use available resources such as balloons, bubbles, simple puzzles, blocks, and interactive books to stimulate the child's interest.

Notably, the chapter stressed the need to embed this engagement throughout daily routines. Using daily tasks such as bath time, the chapter illustrated practical ways parents can foster a secure environment while integrating fun elements to maintain engagement.

In summary, this chapter underscored the pivotal role of engagement in fostering connection and setting the groundwork for more advanced interactions, such as non-verbal communication and gestures, which will be the focus of the next chapter, "Teaching Non-Verbal Communication and Gestures." Here, parents will learn how to guide their children in expressing their needs and emotions effectively without relying on verbal communication.

4

TEACHING NON-VERBAL COMMUNICATION AND GESTURES

You may have heard the statistic that 93% of communication is non-verbal. While researchers continue to debate the accuracy of this figure, the fact remains that most of what we're saying when we interact with others has less to do with our words than we might think. This fact is particularly significant when communicating with children with autism, who may struggle with understanding verbal language but may be more attuned to non-verbal cues.

Therefore, learning to express and interpret non-verbal communication, including body language, tone, gestures, facial expressions, and positioning, is crucial. These elements communicate attention, interest, and emotions and help understand the message beyond words. This chapter will focus on how to teach non-verbal communication and gestures to children with autism. We will explore the benefits of understanding body language and non-verbal cues, explore various teaching strategies, and provide examples of incorporating these lessons into daily activities.

THE IMPORTANCE OF NON-VERBAL COMMUNICATION FOR CHILDREN WITH AUTISM

Non-verbal communication refers to any form of communication that does not involve words. This type of communication is often under-emphasized, yet it plays a significant role in understanding and interpreting information from others. It includes cues such as:

Body language: This involves the way we use our bodies to send signals to others. It includes posture (how we hold and move our bodies), gestures (the movements we make with our hands, arms, and other body parts to express ourselves), and positioning (how we place ourselves in relation to others).

Facial expressions: These are facial changes that communicate our emotional state. A smile, a frown, a raised eyebrow – all can speak volumes about what we're feeling or thinking.

Tone of voice: It's not just what we say, but how we say it. Our voice's tone, pitch, volume, speed, and inflection can carry meanings that the words alone do not convey.

Eye contact: How we look at someone can communicate attention, interest, or various emotions.

In the context of autism, understanding and utilizing non-verbal communication can be challenging. However, it's crucial to help them improve communication skills, build relationships, and navigate social interactions.

COMMON USES OF NON-VERBAL COMMUNICATION

Non-verbal communication is a crucial aspect of daily human interaction and can sometimes convey even more information than words. Below are some examples of how we use non-verbal communication in our everyday lives:

Facial Expressions: A smile can indicate happiness or approval, a frown can express disappointment or concern, and widened eyes might denote surprise or fear. These are universal expressions understood across cultures.

Gestures: Waving goodbye, nodding in agreement, or shaking our heads to signify disagreement are all common gestures we use routinely to communicate without speaking.

Body Posture: Our body position can tell much about our attitudes and emotions. For instance, crossed arms might indicate defensiveness or discomfort, while leaning forward can show interest and engagement in a conversation.

Eye Contact: Making eye contact when someone is speaking is a universal sign of attentiveness and respect. In contrast, avoiding eye contact may be seen as disinterest or discomfort.

Physical Contact: A handshake, a pat on the back, or a hug can communicate a range of feelings, from professional respect to comfort, to affection.

Proximity: The distance we maintain from others can communicate our comfort level, familiarity, and intimacy. For instance, standing too close may be seen as aggressive or intimate, while standing too far away might be viewed as aloof or uninterested.

Tone of Voice: Even without considering the words, the tone of voice can indicate sarcasm, anger, affection, or a multitude of other emotions.

By learning these non-verbal cues, children with autism can gain a deeper understanding of social interactions, helping them form better connections with others and navigate social environments more effectively.

WAYS CHILDREN WITH AUTISM MAY STRUGGLE WITH NON-VERBAL COMMUNICATION

Children with Autism Spectrum Disorder (ASD) often struggle with understanding and interpreting non-verbal communication. It can occur for a variety of reasons, and these challenges manifest in several ways:

Difficulty Recognizing and Interpreting Facial Expressions: Many children with ASD struggle to understand what different facial expressions mean. For example, they may not recognize that a smile signifies happiness or that a frown indicates sadness or displeasure.

Trouble with Eye Contact: Maintaining eye contact during a conversation can be challenging for individuals with ASD. It might be due to overstimulation or discomfort, which can result in seeming disinterested or disengaged.

Issues Understanding Gestures: Simple gestures that most people instinctively understand, such as waving for "goodbye" or nodding for "yes," can be hard to interpret for a child with autism. They may also struggle to use these gestures spontaneously in their own communication.

Struggles with Body Language and Posture: Understanding the subtleties of body language, such as the difference in posture when someone is interested or disinterested, can be particularly challenging. It can lead to difficulties in understanding other people's feelings or intentions.

Misinterpretation of Tone of Voice: Children with ASD often have difficulty interpreting different tones of voice. They might not pick up on the nuances in tone that convey sarcasm, anger, or other emotions.

Difficulty with Personal Space and Proximity: Understanding and maintaining appropriate personal space can be difficult for children with autism. They might stand too close or too far away from others during conversation, leading to discomfort or misunderstanding.

These challenges can create significant barriers to communication and social interaction. However, with appropriate support, strategies, and teaching, children with ASD can learn to better understand and use non-verbal communication, which is essential for their social development and engagement with others.

BENEFITS OF UNDERSTANDING BODY LANGUAGE AND NON-VERBAL CUES SPECIFICALLY FOR CHILDREN WITH AUTISM

Understanding body language and non-verbal cues can offer numerous benefits for children with Autism Spectrum Disorder (ASD), including the following:

Enhanced Social Interactions: Many social interactions are based on non-verbal cues. By understanding these cues, children with ASD can better navigate social situations, forming stronger relationships and friendships.

Improved Emotional Understanding: Non-verbal communication is essential for identifying and interpreting the emotions of others. It can help children with ASD empathize with others and respond appropriately to their feelings.

Increased Independence: Mastering non-verbal communication can lead to greater independence in daily life. For instance, children can better understand instructions, expectations, and environmental cues that aren't explicitly spoken.

Better Communication of Needs and Desires: Non-verbal communication isn't just about understanding others – it's also a valuable tool for expressing oneself. Children with ASD can use non-verbal cues to communicate their needs, feelings, and desires, even if they struggle with verbal communication.

Improved Academic Performance: Many classroom activities rely on non-verbal cues. Understanding these cues can improve a child's academic performance and enhance their classroom experience.

Reduction of Misunderstandings and Frustration: Misunderstanding social cues can lead to frustration and potential conflict. By learning to understand these cues, children with ASD can reduce miscommunication and feel more at ease in social settings.

While understanding non-verbal cues offers many advantages, it's vital to approach teaching in a patient, consistent, and supportive manner. Not all children with ASD will grasp these skills at the same pace, and that's perfectly okay. The goal is steady progress and growth, not immediate perfection.

Understanding non-verbal cues can also significantly influence various areas of development in children with ASD, such as:

Language Development: Non-verbal communication serves as a foundation for language development. Children learn to communicate through gestures, facial expressions, and body language before using words. For children with ASD, understanding non-verbal cues can help pave the way for verbal language acquisition.

Vocabulary Expansion: Even after a child has started using words, non-verbal cues can still enhance their vocabulary. For instance, children learn new words and their meanings by observing others' reactions and interactions. They might understand that "happy" not only means a good feeling but also involves smiling or laughing by observing the facial expressions and body language associated with the word.

Cognitive Development: Non-verbal cues can play a role in cognitive development. For example, understanding gestures can improve a child's ability to solve problems and think critically. By observing how others react to different situations, they can develop cognitive skills like cause-effect understanding, prediction, and inference.

Emotional Expression: Non-verbal communication is crucial for expressing emotions. Children with ASD often struggle to verbalize their feelings, making non-verbal cues even more critical. They can convey their feelings more effectively by learning to use gestures, facial expressions, and body language. For instance, a child might learn to stomp their feet when angry or to hug someone when they're happy.

Incorporating teaching non-verbal cues into a child's routine can be highly beneficial, but it's crucial to do it in a way that suits the child's needs, preferences, and pace of learning. It's also essential to celebrate every small success along the way and reinforce the child's self-confidence.

IN PRACTICE

Imagine a parent and a child with autism playing together. The child is absorbed in lining up a series of toy cars. Instead of redirecting the child to another activity, the parent sits beside the child, catches their eye to ensure they have their attention, and then starts to line up their own cars in the same way. The parent carefully mirrors the child's facial expressions and movements, providing a non-verbal signal that they're participating in the child's world.

Once the parent has successfully entered the child's play, they might add a slight variation to the game. Perhaps the parent begins to move one car up and down as if it's going over a hill, using exaggerated facial expressions and gestures to convey the idea of the car struggling up and then zooming down the hill. The parent looks at the child and smiles, silently inviting the child to do the same.

This non-verbal interaction serves multiple purposes:

- The parent is demonstrating their interest and engagement in the child's activity, strengthening the bond between them.
- The parent is providing a model for the child to imitate, teaching a new way to play with the cars.
- The parent's facial expressions and gestures add an emotional dimension to the play, helping the child to connect their actions with feelings of fun and excitement.

In this way, non-verbal cues and body language not only facilitate communication with a child with autism but also pave the way for teaching new skills and strengthening the emotional connection.

TEACHING BODY LANGUAGE

Teaching non-verbal communication and body language to children with autism is crucial for their overall communication skills. Breaking down this complex process into simple, manageable steps is important. Here are a few strategies and techniques to start with:

The "Do Less" Approach: It might seem counterintuitive, but doing less for your child can help them learn more. In other words, resist the urge to immediately intervene or 'fix' situations. Instead, use body language and non-verbal cues to prompt your child towards a solution. For example, if your child can't open a snack package, instead of instantly opening it, use a gesture to encourage them to try harder or show different ways they can approach the task.

Waiting for a Response: This technique involves using body language or gestures and then waiting for your child to respond. You might need to wait longer than you'd expect. The goal here is to give the child time to process your non-verbal communication and respond appropriately.

Linking Facial Expressions with Emotions: Use books, flashcards, mirrors, or even your own face to teach your child about different facial expressions and their meaning. You can exaggerate expressions for clarity and pair them with the corresponding emotion's name.

Presenting Choices for Responses: This can be an excellent method for teaching non-verbal communication. For example, hold up two food items and ask your child which one they want. They can respond non-verbally by pointing to the preferred item. Presenting choices for responses is an excellent way to develop non-verbal communication and introduce the concept of emotional awareness. In this context, it's not just about teaching the child to choose between two objects but also helping them to express their feelings about their choice. For example, you can hold up a favorite and less-liked toy, asking, "Which one do you want to play with?" Observe their choice and then their emotional reaction. If they select their favorite toy, they might smile, indicating happiness. If they chose the less-liked toy (perhaps by accident), they might frown or look confused. In these moments, you can help your child link their emotions to the choices they make. Say, "You chose your favorite teddy bear! You look happy!" or "You pointed to the red block, but you look upset. Did you mean to choose the blue block?"

Asking for Help: Practice situations where your child needs to ask for help without using words. For instance, place an object in a jar and tighten the lid. Encourage your child to use gestures or facial expressions to communicate their need for help opening it.

Gestures: Teaching children with autism about gestures involves a combination of exaggerated movements and breaking down sequences of gestures. Use exaggerated movements. Since children with ASD often struggle with picking up on subtle social cues, making your movements more pronounced can help them understand what you're trying to convey. This could mean exaggerating a wave goodbye, a thumbs up for a job well done, or a nod to signal agreement. Remember to pair these actions with verbal cues initially so they can associate the gesture with its meaning. For instance, saying "good job" as you give a thumbs up. Break down sequences of gestures. Some gestures involve a series of movements. For instance, waving hello or goodbye is a two-part gesture: you need to raise your hand and then move it side to side. Breaking down these sequences and teaching them in stages can help a child with autism learn them more easily. You can start by guiding your child's hand through the motion while verbally explaining your actions. Over time, encourage them to try on their own until they can perform the gesture independently. Patience is crucial in this process, as it might take several repetitions for your child to understand and mimic these gestures accurately.

These strategies aim to create an interactive environment where non-verbal communication is encouraged. It's important to remember that every child is different, so be patient and persistent. What works for one child might not work for another. Observe your child's reactions and adjust your approach accordingly.

INCORPORATING NON-VERBAL COMMUNICATION INTO DAILY ACTIVITIES

Incorporating non-verbal communication training into daily activities can be a powerful method to help a child with ASD understand and use these cues. Here are a few suggestions:

Morning and Bedtime Routines: Start the day with a wave and a cheerful "Good morning!" As part of the nighttime routine, reinforce the wave as a "good-night" gesture. Gradually, this consistent practice can help your child to understand and start using the waving motion for greetings and goodbyes.

Meal Times: Use gestures such as pointing to items you're discussing, nodding or shaking your head when asking your child if they want a certain food, and showing thumbs up if they like what they're eating. It's also the perfect time to teach them to use sign language for simple words like 'more', 'eat', or 'drink'.

Playtime: Play is a natural way to encourage communication. Use toys to act out scenarios that involve non-verbal communication. For instance, a doll could nod 'yes' or 'no'. Play games that involve non-verbal cues, such as "Simon Says" or "Charades".

Outings and Walks: A trip to the park or a walk around the neighborhood can provide opportunities to point out interesting sights, wave at neighbors, or use facial expressions to show excitement or curiosity.

Story Time: While reading a book together, point to the pictures and use facial expressions and gestures to convey the characters' emotions. Encourage your child to do the same.

Consistency and repetition are key in teaching children with autism non-verbal communication skills. By incorporating this teaching into everyday activities, you can provide your child a natural and comfortable learning environment.

MIMICKING AND IMITATION

One effective strategy to teach non-verbal communication to children with autism is to encourage them to mimic small movements, actions, or gestures. It can be done in a fun and engaging manner during daily routines and playtime. Here's how:

Clapping: Clapping can be taught during moments of joy or achievement. For example, when your child finishes a puzzle or does something correctly, you can clap your hands and say, "Yay! Well done!"

Encourage your child to clap along with you. Use hand-over-hand assistance initially if needed.

Opening Hands: This gesture can be taught while playing with toys or during sensory play. For instance, you could hold a toy in your closed hand and encourage your child to open their hand to receive it. Over time, the child can learn to open their hands to ask for something they want.

Reaching Out Arms: Teach this gesture by reaching out your arms when you want a hug or are about to pick up your child. Initially, you may need to guide their arms to perform the same gesture, but over time, they should start to do this spontaneously when they want to be picked up or given a hug.

Imitation: Children often learn through imitation. You can use this to your advantage by modeling the gestures and facial expressions you want your child to learn. Make sure to exaggerate your movements and expressions to make them more noticeable and easier to imitate.

Hand Over Hand: This technique involves physically guiding the child's hand through the motion of the desired gesture. For example, if you're teaching your child the thumbs-up gesture, you might gently grasp their hand, form it into the thumbs-up shape, and then guide their hand upward. Gradually, as they begin to understand and perform the gesture independently, you can reduce and eventually eliminate your assistance.

It's important to provide plenty of opportunities for your child to practice these gestures in different contexts to help generalize the skills. Also, always remember to reward your child's attempts at using these gestures to reinforce their learning.

This chapter delved into the crucial role non-verbal communication plays for children with Autism Spectrum Disorder (ASD). We began by defining non-verbal communication and its various facets, such as body language, tone, gestures, facial expressions, posture, and positioning. It highlighted the significance of maintaining an attentive, front-and-center position as it facilitates communication of interest and engagement.

We underscored the unique struggles children with ASD face with non-verbal communication. A general overview of how individuals typically use non-verbal communication was presented to underline its importance and to lay a foundation for teaching these skills to children with autism.

The benefits of understanding and using non-verbal cues and body language were discussed in relation to children with autism. These benefits encompass several areas, including language development, vocabulary enhancement, emotional expression, and other areas of improvement.

Several practical examples and strategies were provided to guide parents or caregivers in teaching non-verbal communication to their children. These included presenting choices for responses and linking them to emotions, incorporating exaggerated movements, and breaking down sequences of gestures.

We also explored various ways to integrate non-verbal communication teachings into daily activities. Key techniques were emphasized, such as getting the child to mimic small movements and actions, using a hand-over-hand approach when necessary. The chapter concluded with practical applications of these techniques involving gestures like clapping, opening hands, and reaching out arms.

After exploring non-verbal communication in depth, the next chapter will build upon this knowledge by focusing on "Teaching Imitations." It will include how to encourage children with autism to imitate actions and expressions, a skill critical for their social development and communication skills.

5

TEACHING IMITATIONS

In this chapter, we explore the significance of teaching young children with autism the process of imitation. As a fundamental social skill, imitation carries the powerful message of validation and understanding. By imitating our children's actions, we reinforce their importance to us and foster a deeper bond with them.

Imitation is a powerful tool in communication and inter-personal relationships. It is often said that 'imitation is the sincerest form of flattery.' The truth of this statement becomes evident when we think back to a time when we were imitated by someone else - perhaps they picked up a phrase we often use or emulated a particular way we do things. Those instances likely evoked a sense of validation and understanding, leading us to feel important and recognized.

In the realm of parenting, especially with children with autism, the act of imitation takes on an even deeper meaning. We demonstrate our genuine interest in their world by carefully observing our children and echoing their actions. This action sends them a powerful message - "You matter, and I value your perspective." This act of imitation fosters a bond of mutual respect and understanding, offering a solid foundation for effective communication.

Imitation is a fundamental aspect of communication, particularly in the development of children with Autism Spectrum Disorder (ASD). The capacity to mimic actions, expressions, and sounds is instrumental in fostering communication skills and strengthening bonds with others.

One of the reasons imitation is so vital is that it provides a bridge to social connection. As children mimic the actions and sounds of those around them, they participate in a shared activity, fostering a sense of belonging and understanding. It forms the basis of social interaction and provides a platform for further communication development.

Additionally, imitation encourages language development. Children often learn to say words and construct sentences by repeating what they hear from adults around them. This mimicking of speech sounds is vital to learning to talk and enhancing vocabulary.

In the context of autism, the importance of imitation becomes even more pronounced. Children with ASD often struggle with social interaction and communication, and teaching them to imitate can be a valuable tool in overcoming these challenges.

According to several studies and articles, such as those from the Hanen Centre, UT News, and Alliance ABA Therapy, imitation is a key component in speech development, social skill enhancement, and overall communication advancement for children with ASD. This ability to mirror actions not only aids in verbal communication but also non-verbal communication, assisting in comprehending body language and emotional expression.

To emphasize this point, let's look at some real-world examples shared by parents and caregivers on the Hanen Centre's website. These individuals have built stronger relationships and improved communication with their children with autism through the power of imitation. For instance, one parent shares how imitation games have helped her child communicate better and led to joyous, shared moments of laughter and connection.

The scientific community further supports these experiences with research indicating the immense benefits of imitation for children with autism. A study published in the National Library of Medicine explains how children with ASD who had difficulties with imitation also had severe language deficits. It underlines how closely linked imitation and language development are.

In the following sections, we will delve into practical tips and techniques for encouraging imitation, how it plays into turn-taking in communication, and everyday strategies for fostering these skills.

WHY IMITATION IS IMPORTANT FOR BUILDING COMMUNICATION

As evidenced by numerous accounts on the Hanen Centre's site, the power of imitation can be life-changing for families with a child on the autism spectrum.

Take, for example, the story of a mother and her son, whom we'll call Amy and Ethan for the purpose of this narrative. Amy was at her wit's end, feeling like she could not connect with Ethan, who was then three years old and had been diagnosed with autism. However, after being introduced to the imitation strategy, she began mimicking Ethan's actions and noises during playtime instead of trying to guide him to conform to 'normal' play. This simple shift had profound effects. Ethan started to notice his mother more, engage with her, and even imitate her actions in return. Their play sessions became a time of bonding and communication growth rather than frustration and isolation.

In another account, a father named David tells the story of his daughter, Lisa, who was nonverbal at age four. David used imitation as a way to enter Lisa's world. He started copying her actions, facial expressions, and even her sounds. Over time, Lisa began to respond positively to this approach and started copying David back. It was a monumental step in Lisa's communication skills, as she had always struggled with social interaction. By imitating her, David was able to teach her the fundamental basics of communication and interaction.

In both these cases, parents used imitation as a tool to reach their children in ways they hadn't been able to before. Imitation helped create two-way communication, enabling the children to understand and respond to the social cues they previously missed. Not only did it improve their communication skills, but it also allowed their parents to form a deeper bond with them.

Scientific research robustly supports the anecdotal evidence of the power of imitation in aiding social and communication skill development in children with autism. A study published in the Journal of Autism and Developmental Disorders, accessible through the National Institutes of Health, particularly underscores this importance.

The study emphasizes that imitation is a crucial component in children's early development, as a key tool for social and communicative learning. By observing and replicating others' behaviors, children learn about the world around them and how to interact within it.

It is especially critical for children with autism, who often struggle with social communication. The research found that interventions focusing on teaching imitation skills to children with autism can significantly improve their social-communication skills. It also revealed that these benefits extend beyond imitating actions, with the children also demonstrating a general improvement in other areas of social interaction and communication. For instance, children could maintain eye contact better, take turns, and even use more complex communicative gestures.

The study pointed out that teaching imitation skills should not be reserved for therapy sessions only. Instead, it suggests that integrating imitation into daily activities, such as play, can contribute to more effective and natural learning.

Both real-life experiences and empirical studies strongly affirm that teaching and encouraging imitation can be a valuable strategy for fostering social and communication skills in children with autism. It bridges the gap between them and their social environment, promoting better understanding and interaction.

TIPS FOR ENCOURAGING IMITATION

Social Songs and Fingerplays: Incorporate songs into your everyday routine that involve hand movements or body gestures. For example, singing "If You're Happy and You Know It" can help your child associate the clapping hands action with being happy. Similarly, "The Itsy Bitsy Spider" involves complex finger movements that can improve your child's motor skills while teaching the concept of imitation.

Expanding Play with Toys and Objects: Use toys to teach actions and sounds. For instance, while playing with toy cars, you can imitate the car's sound and its movement. Or, with a toy animal like a cow, you can teach your child to imitate the "moo" sound and pretend to walk like a cow. Over time, your child may start associating the sounds and actions with the corresponding toys and replicate them during play.

Using Facial Expressions and Sounds to Encourage Imitation: Make funny faces, noises, or mimic eating and drinking actions and sounds to engage your child. For example, exaggerating your surprised face when opening a book or making a "mmm" sound when tasting food can stimulate your child to imitate. This practice can also be used to teach emotions. When you display a sad face, explain that you're feeling sad, helping your child link the expression to the feeling.

Gradually Fading Prompts and Encouraging Independent Imitation: Start by guiding your child's actions, like helping them clap their hands during a song. As they begin to understand the action, gradually reduce your physical prompts until they can perform it independently. This process can promote self-confidence and independence in their ability to imitate.

Watch Your Child, Then Imitate Them: Imitation is a two-way street. When you imitate your child's sounds, movements, or play, you validate their actions and provide them with a model for imitating others. It can be as simple as mimicking their excited hand movements or the unique way they play with a particular toy.

Focus on Simple Actions to Replicate: Start with straightforward actions your child sees regularly, like waving goodbye, clapping, or nodding. As their imitation skills improve, you can gradually introduce more complex actions.

Positive Reinforcement When Child Correctly Imitates: Provide immediate positive feedback whenever your child successfully imitates an action or sound. It can be in the form of verbal praise, a hug, or a favorite treat. Positive reinforcement encourages the repetition of the behavior and reinforces the learning process.

Practicing these strategies consistently can significantly improve your child's imitation skills, providing a foundation for better social interaction and communication.

TURN-TAKING AND COMMUNICATION

In the story of Chris, a young man diagnosed with Autism Spectrum Disorder (ASD), we see a clear illustration of how practicing cooperation and turn-taking can lead to significant improvements in social interaction and communication. Chris's story, shared by the Centre for Autism Services Alberta, is an inspiring example of the power of patience, practice, and persistence.

When Chris first started attending the Centre, he found social interaction challenging, especially when it involved cooperation and taking turns. For Chris, like many children with ASD, sharing attention and engaging in activities with others were unnatural and complex tasks.

However, the professionals at the Centre were determined to help Chris improve his social skills. They began working on these areas by introducing cooperative games that encouraged turn-taking, like board games and group sports activities. The activities were chosen carefully to be fun and engaging for Chris, making the learning process feel less like a chore and more like playtime.

Gradually, through consistent practice and positive reinforcement, Chris began to understand the concept of taking turns. His interactions with others improved noticeably. He started to engage more in cooperative play and became more comfortable sharing attention and interacting in a group setting. It was a small but significant victory for Chris and the dedicated team at the Centre.

This success didn't just stay within the Centre's walls. Chris transferred these skills into his daily life, improving his interactions with his family and peers outside the Centre. Today, Chris can maintain conversations, interact with his peers, and participate in social activities that he previously found challenging. He even has a part-time job where he interacts with customers and colleagues.

Chris's story is a testament to the power of teaching turn-taking and cooperation to children with autism. Children like Chris can make enormous strides in social and communication skills with patience, consistency, and creativity. His story serves as inspiration for parents and educators alike, demonstrating that every child has the potential to overcome their challenges and thrive.

Let's take a common scenario many of us have experienced: a group conversation during a dinner party.

Imagine you're at a dinner party where everyone is eager to share their thoughts and experiences. During the lively discussion, one person begins to share a story. However, before they can finish, another person interrupts to share their related experience. The original speaker never gets the opportunity to complete their tale, and the flow of conversation becomes fragmented.

Not only does this scenario create an awkward social situation, but it also undermines the importance of the initial speaker's contribution. It demonstrates a lack of respect for their turn in the conversation and can lead to feelings of frustration or insignificance. For the person interrupted, this may discourage them from sharing in the future, resulting in less meaningful exchanges within the group.

In the context of communication, it's essential to understand and respect the concept of turn-taking. Letting others finish their thoughts before we share ours is a fundamental aspect of effective communication. It fosters a sense of respect and understanding among participants, which is crucial for building strong relationships.

For children with autism, learning this principle can be especially beneficial. They often struggle with social interactions and communication, so understanding the concept of turn-taking can significantly improve their ability to engage in conversations. This, in turn, can enhance their social skills, improve their relationships, and boost their self-esteem.

Turn-taking is an essential social skill that applies to everyone, not just children with autism. In every conversation, be it in personal or professional settings, observing the concept of turn-taking ensures a balanced, respectful, and productive exchange of ideas.

A blog post from MindTools titled "Why People Don't Listen" highlights this principle. It notes how common it is for people to focus on what they will say next, rather than fully paying attention to the person speaking. They may be waiting for a pause to interject their thoughts rather than genuinely listening and responding to the speaker's ideas. This behavior is not just discourteous; it also hinders meaningful and constructive communication.

By highlighting this, we aim to underscore the universality of the turn-taking principle. It's an important communication skill that everyone can improve upon, not just children with autism. Doing so can create a more respectful and understanding society that values each individual's thoughts and contributions. For children with autism, seeing this principle practiced in their everyday lives can help them better understand and implement it, thus improving their social interactions.

Turn-taking in communication is not just a social courtesy; it has been found to significantly benefit language development, particularly in children with autism. Here are a few research-backed benefits of this:

Development of Language Skills: According to an article on the Hanen Centre's website, turn-taking helps activate parts of the brain responsible for language development. This means alternating between listening and responding in a conversation encourages the child to comprehend and respond effectively, thereby developing receptive and expressive language skills.

Promotes Cooperation and Social Interaction:
Studies suggest that turn-taking promotes cooperative behavior. When children with autism understand and practice turn-taking, they learn to share experiences, objects, or activities with others. This process promotes a sense of cooperation and boosts their interaction with peers, an important skill necessary for their social development.

Improves Emotional Understanding: Turn-taking can help children with autism better understand their and others' emotions. It is because it involves the exchange of emotional content, like tone of voice and facial expressions, which can help children recognize and interpret emotional cues.

Promotes Self-Regulation: Waiting for one's turn to speak or play can help develop self-regulation skills. It teaches children the ability to control their impulses, manage their behavior, and adjust to situations, which is particularly beneficial for children with autism who might struggle with these skills.

These benefits don't just apply to verbal communication. Non-verbal interactions such as sharing toys or taking turns in games can also have the same positive impact. The key is to incorporate turn-taking practices in various daily activities to help children with autism understand and adapt this crucial social skill.

Engaging in turn-taking activities has been shown to contribute to language development in children with autism significantly. Researchers have found that turn-taking plays a vital role in triggering the parts of the brain associated with language learning.

It happens because when children take turns, they're not just waiting for their chance to speak or act; they're also listening, processing, and understanding what the other person is saying or doing. This active engagement helps stimulate the language centers in their brain, promoting the acquisition and understanding of new words, phrases, and sentence structures.

The back-and-forth nature of turn-taking supports the development of conversational skills. Children learn to listen to others' thoughts, formulate their responses, and then express them effectively. They learn to comprehend the flow of a conversation and how to contribute meaningfully.

Turn-taking serves as an essential tool for activating and strengthening the language-learning mechanisms in a child's brain, making it an indispensable part of therapy and education for children with autism.

In addition to language skills, turn-taking fosters a sense of cooperation and sharing among children with autism. By nature, turn-taking is a cooperative activity that requires understanding and respect for the other person's time and space. It can significantly aid children with autism in social situations.

Cooperation is a fundamental social skill that forms the basis of successful interpersonal relationships. When children engage in turn-taking activities, they learn to wait for their turn and respect the turn of others, teaching them patience and impulse control. They also learn to anticipate and understand the actions and reactions of their peers, which promotes empathy and understanding.

In activities that involve shared resources, such as playing with toys, turn-taking teaches the concept of sharing. It can be particularly beneficial for children with autism who may initially find it challenging to share their belongings. Gradual exposure to turn-taking can help them understand that sharing doesn't mean losing out but leads to a more enjoyable and enriching play experience.

Teaching turn-taking skills to children with autism can significantly enhance their ability to cooperate with others and share, improving their social interactions and relationships in the long run.

STRATEGIES FOR TEACHING TURN-TAKING ON A DAILY BASIS

Incorporating turn-taking exercises into a child's daily routine can significantly improve their social communication skills. Here are some strategies and tips that you can apply:

Use Toys to Model Turn-Taking: Toys are a great medium to teach children about taking turns. For instance, you can take turns to place a block while building a Lego tower. The key here is to verbalize the turns, saying, "Now, it's your turn," and then, "Now, it's my turn."

Playing Games: Simple games like 'catch' or board games also offer excellent opportunities to practice turn-taking. Say so explicitly when it's the child's turn, and do the same when it's your turn.

Playdates with Other Children: Organize playdates with other children. Interaction with peers often provides natural scenarios for practicing turn-taking. Monitor these situations closely and guide your child when needed.

Use Visual/Non-Verbal Cues: Use hand gestures, body language, or visual prompts like pictures to signify whose turn it is. These cues can benefit children who have difficulty understanding or processing verbal instructions.

Use a Timer: If your child has difficulty waiting for their turn, using a timer can be helpful. It gives a visual representation of the time left for their turn.

Artistic Activities: Artistic activities provide an excellent opportunity to teach and reinforce the concept of turn-taking. Art, by its very nature, is a broad and flexible medium that allows for experimentation and individual expression. Start a project with your child, such as a large painting or a sculpture. Take turns adding elements to the artwork, emphasizing when it's your turn and when it's your child's turn. This shared creative experience teaches turn-taking and fosters a sense of collaboration.Play a game where you take turns adding to a drawing or painting. For example, one person might draw a shape, and then the next person has to add to it, and so on. Make sure to announce whose turn it is each time to reinforce the concept of turn-taking.Engage in craft activities like making a collage or decorating a cardboard box. One person could select and glue the pieces, while the other person can decide where to place them. Take turns performing each role.If your child is interested in music, consider turn-taking activities that involve musical instruments or sounds. You could create a pattern with an instrument or your voice and then have your child imitate it, taking turns to make different sounds or rhythms.Create a story together using drawings or paintings. One person starts by creating a part of the story through their art, and then the other person continues it, and so on.

In this chapter, we delved into the pivotal role of imitation in communication development for children with autism. We began with a compelling success story demonstrating how the simple act of pointing enabled effective communication with a child with autism. Real-life examples further substantiated the significance of imitation, where parents shared how they established stronger bonds and more efficient communication with their children by leveraging this technique.

We referred to several studies underscoring the value of imitation in cultivating social and communication skills among children with autism. We explored various tips and strategies for fostering imitation throughout the day, including social songs and fingerplays, expanding play with toys and objects, using facial expressions and sounds, and gradually encouraging independent imitation.

Turn-taking, another critical aspect of communication, was emphasized, particularly through the narrative of a child with autism who significantly improved his cooperative skills. We related this concept to the universal challenge of active listening, highlighting that everyone, not just children with autism, can benefit from practicing turn-taking. Research-backed benefits of turn-taking, such as language skills development and fostering cooperation, were discussed.

We proposed strategies to inculcate turn-taking in daily life, culminating in the creative domain of artistic activities. These included shared art projects, drawing games, craft activities, music making, and storytelling with art, all designed to reinforce the concept of turn-taking while promoting interaction and creativity.

Having delved into the importance and methods of teaching imitation and turn-taking, in the next chapter, we will explore another key aspect of communication: joint attention. This will involve understanding how to guide your child's attention in a shared activity, strengthening their connection with others and their surroundings.

6

TEACHING JOINT ATTENTION

This chapter explores the significance of teaching young children with autism how to engage in joint attention. As a fundamental social skill, this shared interest carries the powerful message of sharing and understanding. By teaching this valuable tool, we reinforce their connection to us and foster a deeper bond with them.

Joint attention is a powerful tool in communication and interpersonal relationships. We demonstrate our genuine interest in their world by carefully observing our children and engaging with them. This action sends them a powerful message - "You matter, and I value your perspective." It fosters a bond of mutual respect and understanding, offering a solid foundation for effective communication. In the ensuing sections of this chapter, we will explore how we can harness this skill to support our children's development.

Pointing plays a unique role in this regard, serving as a primary exercise to train focus. For children with autism, maintaining focus can be challenging due to their generally shorter attention spans. Teaching children how to point can help bolster their ability to concentrate.

Pointing carries several benefits for the child's development. It encourages joint attention as children learn to show or share objects they find interesting. It also serves as a communication tool when children want to ask for things or seek help. Furthermore, it promotes exploration and curiosity, prompting the child to engage more with their environment.

In the following sections, we will explore practical techniques and tips to teach your child how to point throughout the day. These strategies will include modeling pointing, engaging in games designed for communication, reading picture books together, and leveraging assistive technology. These methods aim to make the learning experience more effective and enjoyable for your child.

CHILDREN WITH AUTISM HAVE A HARD TIME WITH FOCUS

Children with autism often struggle with focus due to various factors, including a shorter attention span. The attention span is the amount of time an individual can maintain focus on a task or activity. For children with autism, this period can be considerably shorter than it is for neurotypical children. This short attention span can make it challenging for them to stay engaged in activities for extended periods and impact their ability to learn new skills or information.

One reason for shorter attention spans in children with autism may be related to their unique sensory experiences. Many children with autism have different ways of processing sensory information - they may be overly sensitive to some types of sensory input or not sensitive enough to others. It can lead to feeling overwhelmed or distracted, making it difficult for them to concentrate.

Children with autism often have specific interests that they are intensely focused on. They might struggle when required to shift their attention from these interests to something else. Their focus can be so narrow and concentrated that it's challenging to redirect their attention to a new or less-preferred activity.

Understanding these challenges is critical to developing strategies and interventions that can help children with autism improve their focus and attention skills. It's essential to remember that each child with autism is unique, and strategies that work for one child might not work for another. Consequently, it's often necessary to try different approaches and find the one that suits the individual child best.

POINTING HELPS TRAIN THE ABILITY TO FOCUS ATTENTION

Pointing plays a significant role in training the focus and attention of children with autism. This simple yet meaningful gesture can significantly contribute to their cognitive, social, and language development.

When a child points to an object or direction, they consciously decide to shift their attention towards it. It requires identifying the object of interest and tuning out other distractions in the environment. In this way, pointing can help train their ability to selectively focus their attention.

Pointing is a shared experience that involves both the child who is pointing and the person to whom the pointing is directed. For instance, when a child points to a toy, it also invites the adult to shift their attention to it. This form of joint attention can help children with autism understand the value of shared focus and social interaction, thereby improving their social communication skills.

Pointing can also encourage children with autism to explore their surroundings more thoroughly. For instance, when a child points to different objects in a room, they must shift their focus from one item to another. It can stimulate their curiosity and urge to explore, extending their attention span.

Pointing also provides a context for adults to reinforce the child's focus behavior. For example, when a child points at a bird, and the adult responds enthusiastically, saying, "Yes, that's a bird! It's flying high in the sky!", the child gets positive reinforcement. It makes them more likely to repeat the behavior, gradually improving their ability to focus and pay attention.

The seemingly simple act of pointing can serve as an effective tool in training the attention and focus of children with autism, paving the way for their improved cognitive and social development.

BENEFITS OF TEACHING HOW TO PROPERLY POINT

Teaching children with autism to point correctly has many benefits, both for their development and their interactions with the people around them. Children can improve developmentally in the following ways:

Promotes Joint Attention: Joint attention is a fundamental social communication skill where two individuals share attention on the same object or event. It is often achieved through pointing. When your child points at an object, it invites you to look at and discuss the same thing. This shared focus forms the basis of meaningful social interactions and helps the child understand that their actions can influence others' attention.

Facilitates Communication and Asking for Help: Pointing is a powerful non-verbal tool for children with autism to express their needs and wants. Instead of getting frustrated or engaging in challenging behaviors when they can't articulate their desires, they can simply point to the object or person they need. It can enhance their self-efficacy and independence.

Encourages Exploration and Curiosity: When a child points at various things in their environment, it's a clear sign of their interest and curiosity. They're exploring their surroundings and seeking more information. Encouraging pointing fosters a sense of curiosity and a desire to learn more about the world around them.

Improves Social Relationships: As children with autism become more adept at pointing, they can more effectively communicate their interests and desires to others. It can lead to more meaningful social interactions and stronger relationships with peers and adults in their lives.

Acts as a Foundation for Further Language Development: Pointing often precedes verbal communication. For example, a child who points to a cookie is likely to learn the word "cookie" faster as they connect the object and its label.

Teaching your child with autism to point properly opens up new avenues for their social, communicative, and cognitive development. A real-life success story can best illustrate the power of pointing as a tool for development. Let's look at the journey of a young child named Lily, whose story is inspired by various accounts of children with autism and their experiences with pointing.

Lily was a lively 3-year-old girl with autism. Like many children with autism, she struggled with expressing her needs and wants. She often experienced meltdowns when she couldn't make herself understood. In their quest to support their daughter, Lily's parents decided to focus on teaching Lily to point as a means to better communicate her needs.

At first, Lily found the concept of pointing challenging. Her parents started by taking her favorite toy, a small, plush elephant, and holding it slightly out of her reach, all the while pointing at it. When Lily reached for the elephant, they helped her extend her index finger to point toward the toy. Lily's parents would then cheer and give her the toy, thus reinforcing the idea that pointing could help her communicate her needs.

Lily's parents continued this exercise with various objects and gradually introduced more distance between Lily and the objects to encourage her to use pointing more actively. They would also imitate Lily's actions, which helped Lily understand the concept of joint attention. For example, if Lily pointed at a bird outside, they would follow her point, look at the bird, and then talk about it with her.

As weeks turned into months, Lily began to point on her own, often with a delightful chuckle. She would point to ask for food, toys, and even to share interesting sights with her parents. The number of her meltdowns reduced significantly as she could now communicate her needs better.

Additionally, Lily's ability to point sparked curiosity and exploration. She started noticing and pointing at things she had previously ignored, like pictures in books or patterns on the curtains. It opened up opportunities for her parents to expand her knowledge and vocabulary.

Lily's story is a powerful testament to the power of pointing as a developmental tool for children with autism. From being a child frustrated by her inability to express herself, Lily became a curious explorer actively engaging with her environment, all thanks to the simple act of pointing.

TEACHING YOUR CHILD TO POINT THROUGHOUT THE DAY

Teaching your child to point can seem like a daunting task, but incorporating this skill into your everyday routines can make the process much smoother. Here are some strategies you can use to help your child learn to point:

Model Pointing: Demonstrating the action is an excellent starting point. Use your index finger to point at things throughout the day while you name them. Focus on items your child shows interest in or needs, like their favorite toy or a snack.Keep repeating. During your daily routines, consistently point out objects, people, or events of interest. For instance, at breakfast, you could point to the cereal box and say, "Look, we're having cereal today." Point to high-desire items and objects. If your child loves a specific toy, use it to guide their pointing. Hold it slightly out of reach and say, "Do you want the teddy?" while pointing at it. It encourages your child to point to express their desire. Start with close items and gradually increase the distance. Begin with objects within arm's reach. As your child becomes adept at this, gradually move to pointing at objects further away. For example, you could progress from pointing at toys on a table to pointing at birds in the garden.

Playing Pointing Games: Interactive games can make learning fun and exciting. You can play "I Spy" or hide and seek with toys and encourage your child to point at the objects when they find them. Try games that involve moving objects, like a ball rolling game. Roll a ball back and forth and each time it's your turn, announce it by saying, "My turn" and pointing to yourself. When it's their turn, say, "Your turn" while pointing at them.

Use Visual Aids: Picture books are an excellent resource for teaching pointing. As you read together, point to the characters, objects, and actions in the book. Pause and encourage your child to do the same.

Associate Actions with Pointing: When playing with toys, point to the toy and describe its action. For example, if you're playing with a toy car, point to it and say "car goes vroom!" Encourage your child to point to the car and imitate its sound.

Reinforce Good Behavior: Provide immediate positive feedback whenever your child points correctly. It could be verbal praise like "Great job pointing at the toy!" or a tangible reward like giving them the toy they pointed at.

Use Assistive Technology: There are several apps designed to foster communication skills in children with autism. Many of these use pointing as a method of interaction. Some apps even allow you to customize the content to include familiar objects and people, making the learning process more personalized and engaging.

Here are other tips with real-world examples of how to apply them:

The Power of Desire: Say you're playing with your child and their favorite toy, perhaps a colorful ball, is just out of their reach. You could say, "Oh look, the ball! Do you want the ball?" while pointing at it. This can encourage your child to point to the toy they want.

Increasing Distance Gradually: Initially, you could be sitting close to a toy shelf and point out various toys asking your child, "Where is the teddy?" As they get comfortable with this, you could gradually move away from the shelf, increasing the distance from which your child has to point.

Interactive Reading: During storytime, while reading a book about farm animals for example, you could point to a cow and say, "Look at the cow. Can you point to the cow?" After they've done this, you can praise them and proceed to the next animal.

Turn-taking Games: Simple games like 'I Spy' can be beneficial. You can start by saying, "I spy with my little eye, something that is red," while pointing at a red item in the room. Then encourage your child to take a turn.

Make Use of Their Interests: If your child loves cars, use this to your advantage. During play, you could point to a car and say, "Look, a red car!" and then encourage your child to point to another car.

Prompting: When starting out, you can gently hold your child's hand, extend their index finger, and guide their hand to point at an object. For example, "Let's point to the cat," while guiding their hand towards the pet.

Be Patient and Positive: Suppose your child has just pointed at a toy for the first time, though they may not have extended their index finger fully. You can say, "Great job! You pointed at the teddy," to provide positive reinforcement for their effort.It may take some time for your child to learn to point, but with persistent effort, they will gradually master this valuable skill.

In this chapter, we delved into the importance and benefits of teaching children with autism how to point and how it can significantly enhance their communication skills. We started by exploring why imitation is critical in communicating and connecting with children with autism, highlighting how it can make them feel validated and important.

We then discussed the challenges children with autism often face when it comes to focusing, particularly noting their generally shorter attention spans. We uncovered the instrumental role that pointing can play in training and improving their ability to focus attention, using various practical examples to solidify our explanations.

We evaluated the manifold benefits of teaching children to point correctly. These benefits ranged from facilitating joint attention and asking for help, to promoting exploration and curiosity. Each of these benefits was backed up with real-life success stories, underscoring the tangible, positive impact such strategies can have on the development of a child with autism.

Turning to practical application, we suggested various tips and techniques parents can use to teach their children how to point. We provided concrete examples for applying each tip, encompassing modeling pointing, playing games beneficial for pointing, reading picture books, reinforcing good behavior, and making use of assistive technology.

By the end of the chapter, the importance of pointing as a critical communication tool for children with autism became clearly evident. However, developing these skills is just one part of the communication puzzle. In the upcoming chapter, we'll expand our focus to include building expressive language skills, a vital next step in fostering even more effective communication for children with autism.

7

BUILDING RECEPTIVE AND EXPRESSIVE LANGUAGE

Opening the chapter, we reflect upon a profound statement by Dr. Stephen Shore: "If you've met one person with autism, you've met one person with autism." This quote serves as a reminder of the unique nature of every individual with autism, emphasizing the need for personalized approaches when teaching them expressive speech and language. This chapter will provide simple techniques and strategies that can help children with autism develop their expressive and receptive language abilities, enhancing their overall communication skills. We understand that every child is different, and so the techniques discussed should be adjusted to suit your child's unique needs.

TEACHING RECEPTIVE LANGUAGE AND COMMANDS

Teaching receptive language and commands to children with autism involves a two-step process: giving commands while assisting the child to follow through, then gradually fading out the prompts. This method revolves around the concept of "hand-over-hand" guidance and the gradual removal of support as the child begins to understand and respond independently.

Hand-over-hand is a technique where the parent or caregiver physically guides the child's hand to perform a task. For instance, if the command is "pick up the toy," you would take your child's hand and guide it to pick up the toy while repeating the command. This technique provides tactile and visual cues for the child, allowing them to connect the command with the action.

Over time, as the child becomes more familiar with the commands, you begin to fade out these prompts. This fading process might start with reducing the physical guidance until the child is just touching the toy. Eventually, the child might start reaching for the toy as soon as you give the command, and at that point, you might eliminate physical guidance entirely. You would continue to monitor their progress and adjust the level of assistance as necessary.

This approach helps the child understand various commands and teaches them to respond appropriately.

Remember, the goal is gradually enabling the child to perform these tasks independently, enhancing their receptive language skills. Each child's pace will differ, so patience and consistency are key.

WHAT IS "EXPRESSIVE" COMMUNICATION

In the field of language and communication, two key terms are often used: receptive communication and expressive communication. Understanding these two terms is crucial to grasping how we process and produce language, especially in the context of autism.

Receptive Communication: This refers to our ability to understand information being shared with us, essentially the 'input' or 'listening' aspect of communication. Receptive communication involves decoding and making sense of spoken words, gestures, signs, or written words. For instance, when someone speaks to us, we listen, process the information, and understand what is being said. When we read a book, we're receiving and understanding written language. For a child with autism, receptive communication skills could include understanding simple commands, recognizing pictures, or following a story being read to them.

Expressive Communication: This refers to how we convey our thoughts, feelings, and ideas to others, making it the 'output' or 'talking' aspect of communication. Expressive communication can be spoken words, written words, signs, gestures, or facial expressions. For example, when we're having a conversation, writing an email, or using sign language, we're using expressive communication. In the context of a child with autism, expressive communication skills could involve requesting a toy, commenting on an activity, or responding to a question.

While these two types of communication are different, they are closely connected and often work hand in hand. For example, a conversation (a common form of communication) requires us to listen to the other person (receptive communication), process what they've said, and then respond appropriately (expressive communication). In the journey of helping a child with autism improve their communication skills, it's essential to consider both receptive and expressive communication, as they are integral to interacting effectively with others.

While the words we use in communication certainly hold weight, there's a myriad of other factors that contribute to the actual meaning that's conveyed in our interactions. It is especially important when dealing with individuals with autism who might experience communication differently. Other aspects of communication interpretation include:

Nonverbal Communication: Nonverbal cues like facial expressions, body posture, gestures, eye contact, touch, and even our distance from the listener play a huge role in how our message is interpreted. For instance, a broad smile can indicate joy or approval, a frown can signal displeasure or confusion, and an eye roll can signify annoyance or disbelief. Nonverbal cues can sometimes speak louder than words.

Paralinguistic Features: These are the variations in speech such as pitch, tone, speed, and volume, that provide additional context to our words. For example, saying "Great job" with a sarcastic tone can change the meaning from a compliment to a criticism.

Context: The situation or setting in which the communication is happening can significantly affect the meaning that's conveyed. The same sentence can have a different meaning in a different context. For example, "Can you pass me the salt?" at a dinner table is a simple request, but in a scientific lab, it might refer to conducting an experiment.

Social Norms: Understanding cultural or social norms is crucial to effective communication. It can include knowing when it's appropriate to speak, understanding shared meanings, or the use of polite language.

Emotional State: The emotional state of the communicator can also affect the message being conveyed. If someone is upset or excited, it may influence their choice of words, their tone, and their nonverbal communication.

In teaching expressive and receptive communication to a child with autism, it's important to consider these aspects as well. For instance, integrating nonverbal communication with verbal instruction can help clarify meaning. Also, using consistent tone and simple language can assist in conveying messages more effectively. It's all about adapting the communication method to meet the child's needs.

Let's consider some everyday adult situations that illustrate how communication extends far beyond words:

During a Business Meeting: In a business meeting, nonverbal cues often hold as much weight as what's being spoken. For example, a team leader leans back in their chair and crosses their arms while another member presents an idea. The leader's posture signals disinterest or disagreement despite not uttering a single word. Similarly, if someone is speaking rapidly or loudly, it could indicate excitement or stress, even if their words are neutral.

In a Romantic Relationship: Imagine a couple having dinner. One partner says "I'm fine" but avoids eye contact, has a stiff posture, and uses a cold tone. Despite the words being said, their nonverbal cues and tone suggest they are anything but fine.

At a Social Gathering: At a party, you notice a friend standing in a corner, not engaging with anyone. Their body language—downcast eyes, folded arms— speaks volumes about their discomfort or desire to be alone, even without them saying a word.

During a Job Interview: An interviewee maintains steady eye contact, offers a firm handshake, and uses a confident tone. These nonverbal behaviors communicate self-assuredness and professionalism, augmenting the impact of their verbal responses.

Teaching a Class: A teacher asks her class, "Does everyone understand?" She observes her students' facial expressions and body language for feedback. Some students might nod enthusiastically while others look away or frown, providing her with nonverbal responses that might be more accurate than if they simply said, "Yes."

In all these scenarios, nonverbal cues, tone, context, and emotional state significantly influence the conveyed meaning. Communication, therefore, isn't just about the words we use, but how we use them and in what context.

Children with autism often express themselves differently than their neurotypical peers due to unique characteristics of their neurological development. These differences can occur in both verbal and non-verbal communication. Here are some examples:

Verbal Communication: Some children with autism might have delayed speech or not speak at all, while others may possess extensive vocabularies and speak in complete sentences. Their tone of voice might be flat and emotionless or overly formal. They might use repetitive phrases or scripts from their favorite shows, a phenomenon known as echolalia. Others may speak about their specific interests at length, even if it's not relevant to the conversation at hand.

Non-verbal Communication: Many children with autism may express themselves through non-verbal cues. It could involve unique body movements, like flapping hands when excited or rocking back and forth when anxious. They might also use objects to communicate their needs, like bringing a cup to indicate thirst.

Facial Expressions and Eye Contact: Children with autism might not use or understand typical facial expressions. They may have trouble maintaining eye contact, which is often a significant part of conventional communication. Their facial expressions might not match what they or others are saying.

Visual Supports: Some children with autism effectively use visual supports, like Picture Exchange Communication System (PECS) cards or digital communication apps, to express their needs, feelings, and thoughts. These systems can be beneficial for non-verbal children or those with significant speech delays.

Behavior as Communication: Sometimes, children with autism express their needs, wants, or feelings through their behavior. It can include self-soothing behaviors, like hand-flapping or spinning, or even challenging behaviors, like tantrums or aggression. For instance, a child might throw a tantrum to express frustration or overwhelm because they find it difficult to express those feelings verbally.

Sensory Responses: Some children with autism might respond or react intensely to sensory stimuli as a form of expression. It could involve seeking specific sensory experiences, like the feeling of certain fabrics, or avoiding others, like loud noises or bright lights.

Recognizing and understanding these different modes of expression is key to communicating effectively with a child with autism. It allows parents, caregivers, and teachers to understand their needs and emotions better and provides a foundation for helping them learn more effective communication strategies.

One of the most fundamental principles in nurturing communication in children with autism is to allow them to find their own mode of expression. This principle recognizes the individuality of each child and their unique ways of understanding and interacting with the world.

Every child with autism is unique, and they will have their preferred methods of communication. For some, it may be verbal, while for others it may be non-verbal cues or visual aids. Still, others might communicate best through written language or through digital communication tools.

The objective is not to impose a specific method of communication on them but to discover and nurture their preferred method. This helps to make communication a positive and meaningful experience for the child. It's about recognizing their strengths and working with them rather than trying to mold them into a one-size-fits-all approach.

For instance, if a child finds comfort and is more expressive through art, it would be beneficial to encourage this form of self-expression and find ways to incorporate it into their communication efforts. Similarly, suppose a child communicates more efficiently through a digital communication app. In that case, the focus should be on mastering and expanding on this tool, rather than forcing them to communicate in a less natural or comfortable way.

This approach respects the individuality of each child with autism, honors their personal experience, and paves the way for more genuine and successful communication. It's about enabling them to express themselves in the most comfortable and effective ways, thus giving them a greater sense of agency and confidence in their ability to interact with the world around them.

Teaching children with autism to be both expressive and receptive in their communication has numerous advantages. Here are some key benefits:

Enhancement of Joint Attention: Joint attention, the shared focus of two individuals on an object or activity, is a critical aspect of communication and social development. Teaching children with autism to be expressive and receptive improves their ability to engage in joint attention, facilitating more meaningful interactions.

Enabling Choice-Making: Expressive and receptive language skills allow children with autism to make their needs, preferences, and decisions known. It enhances their autonomy and fosters a sense of self and self-efficacy.

Improved Ability to Follow Directions: By developing their receptive language skills, children with autism better understand and follow directions. It supports their ability to participate in various activities in school, therapy, or at home.

Increased Social Interaction: As children become more skilled at expressing themselves and understanding others, they can initiate and maintain interactions more effectively. It leads to improved social relationships and reduces feelings of isolation.

Boost in Confidence: With improved communication abilities, children can express their thoughts, feelings, and needs more accurately. It leads to increased self-confidence and encourages further communication.

Enhanced Learning Opportunities: Receptive and expressive language skills form the basis for more complex cognitive and linguistic skills. The more children can understand and communicate, the more they can learn from their environment.

Reduced Challenging Behaviors: Many challenging behaviors in children with autism arise from communication difficulties. The need for these behaviors often decreases as they learn more functional ways to express their needs and understand others.

STRENGTHENING CONNECTION WITH THE POWER OF WORDS

Building communication skills, particularly for children with autism, starts with the basics: conveying fundamental needs and wants. This initial step is crucial as it forms the basis for more complex forms of communication later on.

Children typically begin to communicate because they have a desire or need they want to express. It could be anything from feeling hungry, wanting a particular toy, needing help, or expressing discomfort. At the most basic level, communication is about expressing these needs and wants and being understood by others.

For children with autism, this fundamental stage of communication can present unique challenges. They may struggle to understand how to express their needs or decipher the responses of others. Therefore, teaching them to convey these essential needs and wants becomes the first critical step in building their communication skills.

This initial communication might not be in words. For instance, a child could use gestures, pointing, or leading an adult by the hand to an object or activity they want. What's important is that they're learning to express themselves and initiate communication, laying the foundation for more sophisticated language skills in the future. This fundamental stage is crucial in empowering the child to express their needs and wants, fostering independence and a sense of control over their environment.

MASLOW'S HIERARCHY OF NEEDS

Maslow's Hierarchy of Needs is a psychological theory proposed by Abraham Maslow in 1943, presenting a five-tier model of human needs, often depicted as hierarchical levels within a pyramid. The model begins with the most basic needs at the base, with each level above addressing a more complex need. The levels, from bottom to top, are physiological, safety, love and belonging, esteem, and self-actualization.

When relating this model to communication in children with autism, we can look at the basic or fundamental needs corresponding to the bottom tiers of Maslow's pyramid.

The first level, physiological needs, includes the most basic needs for survival, such as food, water, warmth, and rest. If we think about communication as a means to satisfy these needs, we can understand why the first step in communication is often about expressing these basic needs. For a child, this might be expressing hunger, thirst, or tiredness.

The second level, safety needs, refers to security and safety. For a child with autism, communication can be a tool to express when they feel unsafe or anxious, helping them to establish a sense of security.

As we move up the hierarchy, the needs become more complex, but the foundational communication skills built around expressing basic needs continue to play a crucial role. In fact, effective communication becomes even more important as children with autism learn to navigate social relationships, gain esteem and confidence, and ultimately strive toward self-actualization.

In essence, Maslow's hierarchy provides a framework that helps illustrate why focusing on fundamental needs is a practical starting point when teaching children with autism to communicate. It's about setting up the building blocks for more complex communication and interpersonal skills.

FUNCTIONAL COMMUNICATION TRAINING (FCT) AND THE FIRST LEVEL OF BUILDING COMMUNICATION SKILLS

Functional Communication Training (FCT) is a common and effective approach used in the field of applied behavior analysis (ABA) to help individuals develop effective communication skills. FCT is particularly beneficial for children with autism who may struggle with expressing their needs and wants verbally.

FCT works by identifying the purpose or function of a child's challenging behavior—such as hitting, screaming, or self-harm—and then teaching a more appropriate communication behavior that serves the same function. For example, if a child throws a tantrum because they want a toy, FCT would involve teaching them to use words, sign language, or a communication device to ask for the toy instead.

By focusing on the first level of building communication skills, FCT aligns with the principles of Maslow's hierarchy of needs, addressing fundamental needs and wants. The technique allows children to communicate their most basic needs in a socially appropriate way, which serves as a stepping stone to more complex communication skills. FCT aims to replace challenging behaviors with positive communication skills, which can significantly enhance a child's quality of life and social interactions.

Using Functional Communication Training (FCT) to communicate with children with autism is a systematic process. Here are the basic steps:

Identify the Behavior and Its Function: Start by observing the child's challenging behaviors, such as tantrums, aggression, or self-injury. The goal is to understand the purpose these behaviors serve. What is the child trying to communicate? Is it a desire for a particular toy? A need for attention? The want to escape a task? This step involves careful observation and sometimes a functional behavior assessment (FBA) conducted by a professional.

Select an Appropriate Communication Response:
Once you understand the function of the challenging
behavior, select a replacement behavior that serves
the same function but is more appropriate. It could
be a word, a sign, or using a picture exchange
communication system (PECS). The chosen response
should be simple and easy for the child to learn
and use.

Teach the New Communication Response: Use
consistent, structured teaching strategies to help the
child learn the new communication response. It
might involve modeling the response, guided practice, and lots of positive reinforcement when the
child uses the new response.

Prompt the New Communication Response: When
the child may resort to challenging behavior, prompt
the new communication response. It could be done
verbally, physically, or visually, depending on what
works best for the child.

Reinforce the New Communication Response:
Provide immediate and meaningful reinforcement
when the child uses the new communication
response. It might be giving the child what they
asked for or providing praise, a hug, or a favorite
activity.

Fade Prompts and Support: Over time, gradually reduce the level of prompting and support as the child becomes more adept at using the new communication response. This helps to foster independence.

Generalize the New Skills: Help the child apply this new communication skill across different settings and with different people. Practice at home, at school, and in other environments where the child needs to communicate.

STRATEGIES FOR TEACHING EXPRESSIVE AND RECEPTIVE COMMUNICATION

When it comes to building expressive and receptive language in children with autism, several strategies can be highly effective. Below are a few key approaches:

Simplify Your Language: Use short, clear sentences that match the child's language level. This can make it easier for them to understand and learn new words and phrases.

Visual Cues and Supports: Pictures, signs, and visual schedules can support verbal instructions and messages, making them easier for the child to understand and follow. This helps in building both expressive and receptive communication.

Use the Child's Name Often: Using the child's name before giving instructions can help to capture their attention, which is essential for improving receptive language.

Announce Activities: Narrating the day's activities can reinforce language associated with routine events. For instance, you might say, "Now we're brushing our teeth," or "Let's put on your shoes."

Repeat Functional Words: Focus on key words that are important in the child's daily life. Repeated exposure to these words helps reinforce their meaning and usage.

Narrate Their Actions: Comment on what the child is doing as if you're narrating a movie. This can help them connect actions with words, boosting their receptive and expressive language skills.

Music and Songs: Using music, songs, and rhymes can be a fun way to teach new words and phrases. The rhythmic nature of songs can make language easier to remember.

Confirm Understanding: Ask the child to repeat or demonstrate their understanding of instructions or information. This can help to reinforce receptive language skills.

Turn-Taking Games: Games that require turn-taking can teach children the back-and-forth nature of communication. It can help improve both expressive and receptive skills.

Positive Reinforcement: Always praise the child's attempts to communicate, even if they're not entirely successful. This can boost their confidence and encourage further attempts.

As always, the goal isn't to force the child to communicate in a specific way but to find the best methods for them.

This chapter delved into the intricate processes of developing receptive and expressive language in children with autism. We began by outlining the concept of giving commands and aiding children in following through with these using techniques like hand-over-hand prompting, emphasizing the gradual reduction of such prompts.

We then broke down the receptive and expressive communication concepts, simplifying them to the ideas of 'input' or 'listening' and 'output' or 'talking.' We further expounded on the importance of understanding that communication transcends the boundaries of verbal expression, encapsulating a more profound conveyed meaning.

We provided examples from daily adult interactions to bring these concepts to life, demonstrating how communication stretches beyond mere words. We recognized the unique ways children with autism express themselves, advocating for a child-centered approach that allows them to find their positive mode of expression rather than imposing a pre-set standard.

As we explored the benefits of teaching children with autism to be expressive and receptive, we found how it enhances joint attention, empowers them to make choices, improves their focus and direction-following, promotes interactions with others, and builds confidence. Furthermore, we identified how these skills, in combination with other developmental skills, can foster the child's ability to start talking and communicating more effectively.

We discussed Maslow's hierarchy of needs as the foundational communication structure, focusing on satisfying fundamental needs. We introduced the idea of Functional Communication Training (FCT), a methodology used to help children express their basic needs and wants. We walked through the key steps of FCT, focusing on identifying a child's specific tendencies, determining their communicative intentions, teaching functional expressions, and gradually removing prompts.

Finally, we shared various strategies to enhance expressive and receptive communication. These included simplifying language, using visual cues, incorporating the child's name in communication, narrating daily activities, emphasizing functional words, and leveraging music for learning.

As we move forward to the next chapter, we will delve into expanding your toolkit. We will explore additional therapies and resources that can be beneficial in aiding a child with autism, building upon the foundational skills we have explored in this chapter.

8

EXPANDING YOUR TOOLKIT: ADDITIONAL THERAPIES AND RESOURCES

While the strategies and techniques we've detailed thus far have the potential to significantly enhance your child's development and strengthen your bond with them, they are but a single element of a much larger, multifaceted puzzle. Autism, by its very nature, demands an individualized approach, as every child is unique, and their needs vary. Consequently, diverse therapies, treatments, and resources exist, each with the potential to offer immense benefits for children with autism. As we delve into this chapter, we will be casting our gaze upon these alternative strategies, thereby expanding your toolkit in support of your child's growth and learning.

EFFECTIVE TYPES OF THERAPY FOR CHILDREN WITH AUTISM

Autism is a spectrum disorder, which can manifest in various ways, with differences in symptoms, severity, and impact on each child. Consequently, there isn't a one-size-fits-all approach to therapies and treatments for autism. Just as every child on the autism spectrum is unique, so should be their treatment plans.

Multiple methods of treatment and therapy are effective for children with autism, each targeting different aspects of development and functioning. These methods range from behavior-based to developmental approaches, and even socio-relational approaches, each with unique advantages and focal points.

What's more, these different approaches aren't mutually exclusive. In many instances, a combination of therapies are utilized to address various aspects of a child's development. This multidimensional approach can help create a comprehensive and personalized plan that caters to your child's specific needs, strengths, and interests, ultimately fostering their growth and development in the most optimal way.

In the following sections, we will delve into some of these therapy types, detailing how they work, their benefits, and tips for finding relevant practitioners. With this knowledge, you will be equipped to explore and choose the therapeutic approaches that best align with your child's unique needs and circumstances.

Determining the most suitable therapy or combination of treatments for a child with autism largely depends on the child's individual needs, abilities, and challenges. There is no 'one-size-fits-all' therapy because autism encompasses a wide range of conditions represented by challenges with social skills, repetitive behaviors, speech, and communication.

Every child on the autism spectrum has a unique set of strengths and weaknesses. Some children may have difficulty with social interaction but have strong verbal skills, while others may be nonverbal but have a great capacity for understanding and relating to others. Additionally, the presence of co-existing conditions such as ADHD, anxiety, or sensory processing issues may also influence the choice of therapy.

The child's age and developmental level are also crucial factors in choosing the most effective therapy. For example, younger children or those at earlier developmental stages may benefit more from play-based therapies, while older children or those at more advanced stages might find cognitive-behavioral therapy more beneficial.

Lastly, the choice of therapy should align with the goals of the child and their family. Different therapies have different objectives, from improving communication and social skills to reducing problematic behaviors or fostering independence. When deciding on a therapeutic approach, the family's values, lifestyle, and resources should also be considered.

Given all these factors, working with a multidisciplinary team of professionals who can assess your child's needs and recommend the most appropriate therapies is essential. Remember, your ultimate goal is to enhance your child's quality of life and ability to participate in everyday activities at home, school, and in the community. The most successful therapy will be tailored to your child's unique needs and promotes their strengths.

TYPES OF THERAPY

As we venture further in our journey, we will explore a spectrum of effective therapeutic approaches for children with autism. The beauty of these therapies is that they are not one-size-fits-all but can be uniquely tailored to address your child's individual needs. You may find that one approach resonates more with your child, or a combination of several therapies might work best. Let's delve into some of the most popular types of therapies and see how they operate, the benefits they provide, and some tips to find relevant practitioners.

Applied Behavior Analysis (ABA): ABA is a scientifically validated approach that uses principles of learning and motivation to bring about meaningful and positive changes in behavior. The therapy involves breaking down complex skills into smaller, teachable parts and reinforcing appropriate behaviors. It can help improve communication, social skills, and learning skills while decreasing problematic behaviors. ABA therapists use individualized assessment methods to understand a child's strengths and weaknesses and tailor the therapy to meet their specific needs.

Example: If a child has difficulty with transitions, the therapist may use a visual schedule and timers to provide clear expectations and structure. Gradual exposure and reinforcement can help the child become more comfortable with transitions over time.

Cognitive Behavioral Therapy (CBT): CBT is a type of talk therapy that can help children with autism understand and manage their thoughts and feelings. It can be particularly effective for dealing with anxiety and mood disorders often associated with autism. The therapy focuses on identifying unhelpful thinking patterns, understanding how these thoughts influence emotions and behavior, and developing coping strategies.

Example: If a child becomes extremely anxious about making mistakes, a CBT therapist may help them recognize their fear, challenge their thoughts about perfection, and practice coping strategies such as deep breathing or positive self-talk.

Pivotal Response Treatment (PRT): PRT is a type of behavioral therapy that focuses on targeting key areas of development such as motivation, self-management, and social initiations. The goal is to produce broad improvements across other areas of functioning. PRT uses naturalistic teaching techniques, meaning the learning occurs in a play-based, child-initiated context.

Example: If a child shows interest in a toy car, the therapist will use that toy as a basis for the session, incorporating lessons on sharing, communication, and other social skills.

Occupational Therapy (OT): OT helps children improve their sensory processing skills, fine and gross motor skills, and daily living skills. Occupational therapists can help children with autism learn to perform everyday tasks (like brushing teeth or dressing), engage in play activities, and participate in school and social situations.

Example: If a child struggles with handwriting, the occupational therapist might work on strengthening their fine motor skills through play-based activities like bead threading or play dough manipulation.

Speech and Language Therapy: This therapy aims to improve a child's communication skills, including their ability to understand and use language. Speech therapists can help children with autism with verbal and nonverbal communication, such as using gestures, improving articulation, or assistive communication devices.

Example: If a child is nonverbal, a speech therapist may introduce a picture exchange communication system (PECS) where the child uses pictures to express their needs and wants.

Physical Therapy (PT): PT helps children develop the basic motor skills needed for everyday tasks and play. It can improve their balance, coordination, and strength. Physical therapists can also help with motor planning issues often seen in children with autism.

Example: If a child has difficulties with coordination, the physical therapist may design exercises and activities to improve their ability to navigate their environment safely.

Play Therapy: Play therapy uses play, a natural activity for children, to help them express their feelings, develop social skills, and understand their experiences. It can be beneficial for children with autism to practice social interactions and emotional regulation in a structured but enjoyable context.

Example: A therapist might use role-playing games to help a child practice taking turns, sharing, and dealing with disappointment or conflict.

Each of these therapies offers a unique approach to addressing the challenges associated with autism. The most effective treatment plan often involves a combination of these therapies tailored to the child's needs.

HELPFUL RESOURCES FOR PARENTS

As we explore the world of autism therapies, we must acknowledge that this journey isn't one you need to walk alone. A wealth of resources is available for parents and caregivers advocating for a child with autism. These resources can offer everything from information and insights about autism, practical strategies for daily living, to advocacy and support systems. In this section, we'll provide you with a curated list of helpful resources, briefly describe what each offers, and how they can aid you in enhancing your child's developmental journey.

LIST OF AUTISM APPS

The Autism Parenting Magazine provides a compiled list of the best apps that are designed to aid children with autism. These apps cover a broad spectrum of needs, from language development, social skills training, to daily routine management. They offer interactive ways to help your child build skills, communicate, and learn in a format that's engaging and accessible. Whether you're seeking a tool for skill-building, communication support, or even leisure activities, this list can serve as a valuable starting point for finding apps tailored to the specific needs and interests of your child. Check it out here: https://www.autismparenting magazine.com/best-autism-apps/

ADVOCACY AND INFORMATION

Family Outreach is a fantastic resource for families navigating the world of autism. They offer a variety of resources including support services, information, and importantly, a curated list of grant opportunities. These grants can provide financial assistance for families needing help to access therapies, treatments, and equipment necessary for their child's development. The organization's dedication to uplifting families impacted by autism makes it an invaluable tool for those seeking financial support and more. You can explore their grant links here: https://www.familyoutreach. org/grant-links/

Danny's Wish is an organization dedicated to providing life-enhancing resources and experiences for children and families living with autism and autism spectrum disorders. One of their main initiatives is the iPads for Autism program, which aims to provide free iPads to those with autism as a tool to improve their communication and learning abilities. iPads have been recognized as effective learning tools for children with autism, enabling them to interact with the world around them in ways that may not have been possible otherwise. You can learn more about their programs and how they might benefit your child here: https://dannyswish.org/

Autism Navigator is an innovative online platform that offers a unique collection of web-based tools and courses specifically designed to bridge the gap between science and community practice. The platform uses extensive video footage to present effective evidence-based practices used in natural everyday settings. It offers resources for families, service providers, and professionals, offering a wealth of information on topics such as early signs of autism, how to interact with children on the spectrum, and a comprehensive course on improving early detection and intervention. You can access this valuable resource here: https://autismnavigator.com/

The Association for Science in Autism Treatment (ASAT) is a not-for-profit organization that aims to improve the education, treatment, and care of people with autism. ASAT is committed to providing a clear voice advocating for the use of science-based treatments and combating unvalidated, unsupported, and potentially harmful interventions. They provide a comprehensive website that offers research summaries on a full range of treatments, helpful tips for parents, resources for professionals, and information about the importance of science in autism treatment. You can explore more about ASAT here: https://www.asatonline.org/

The Council of Parent Attorneys and Advocates (COPAA) is an independent, nonprofit organization of parents, attorneys, advocates, and related professionals. COPAA members work to protect the legal and civil rights of students with disabilities and their families. Their primary goal is to secure high-quality educational services and to promote excellence in advocacy. Their website offers resources such as training and webinars, a directory of resources to find advocates and attorneys, and materials to guide parents in understanding and navigating special education law. You can learn more about COPAA here: https://www.copaa.org/

The Autism Society is one of the leading voices in the autism community, dedicated to improving the lives of all affected by autism. They focus on areas of advocacy, information & support, education, and building inclusive communities. The Autism Society's website offers a wealth of resources including an extensive database of autism resources, guidance on navigating an autism diagnosis, and information on current autism research. They also provide a platform for people in the autism community to connect and support each other. Visit the Autism Society here: https://autismsociety.org/

FEDERAL/GOVERNMENT-FUNDED ORGANIZATIONS

The Early Childhood Technical Assistance Center (ECTA) is designed to support state Part C and Section 619 programs in developing high-quality early intervention and preschool special education service systems, increasing local implementation of evidence-based practices, and enhancing outcomes for young children with disabilities and their families. This resource is comprehensive and gives guidance on a range of topics from policy and finance to effective practices and service delivery. Parents can access a wealth of information, resources, and support on this site to help them navigate the world of early intervention. Visit the Early Childhood Technical Assistance Center here: http://ectacenter.org/

The IRIS Center, a part of Vanderbilt University, provides a wide range of free resources about evidence-based instructional and intervention practices. The resources are designed to help educators, administrators, and parents effectively teach and support all learners, particularly struggling learners and those with disabilities. The site offers modules, case studies, activities, and much more on a variety of topics including behavior, autism, differentiated instruction, and assessment, among others. It is a valuable resource for parents looking to better understand and support their child's educational journey. Visit the IRIS Center here: https://iris.peabody.vanderbilt.edu/

The Center for Parent Information and Resources (CPIR) is a comprehensive resource for parents with children who have special needs. The CPIR offers a wealth of information and materials for families, including information about specific disabilities, research-based educational practices, and links to state and local resources. It also includes resources about your rights and protections under the Individuals with Disabilities Education Act (IDEA). The center's main goal is to connect parents with the resources and support they need to make informed decisions about their child's education and development. Visit the Center for Parent Information and Resources here: http://www.parentcenterhub.org/

The Center on Technology and Disability (CTD) is a valuable resource for parents of children with autism and other disabilities. The CTD provides a wealth of information on how technology can enhance the educational experiences and life of individuals with disabilities. Their resources cover a wide array of technology-related topics, including assistive technology, technology-enhanced learning, and how technology can support communication, independence, and inclusion. Specific to autism, they provide resources on topics like how to use technology to improve communication, social interactions, and learning outcomes for children with autism. Visit the Center on Technology and Disability here: http://www.ctdinstitute.org/search/site/autism

In the final chapter, we broadened our perspective. We looked beyond the techniques and strategies discussed so far to explore additional therapies and resources that could further aid in the development of children with autism.

We started the chapter by emphasizing that the approach we discussed throughout the book is just one piece of a larger puzzle. Understanding that there are many therapies and treatments available for children with autism, we introduced some of these methods, explaining that the selection of a particular therapy largely depends on the child's individual needs.

Delving into the popular types of therapy, we looked at behavior-based approaches such as Applied Behavior Analysis (ABA), Cognitive Behavioral Therapy (CBT), and Pivotal Response Treatment. We also discussed developmental approaches like Occupational Therapy, Speech and Language Therapy, and Physical Therapy, as well as socio-relational approaches like Play Therapy.

The second half of the chapter was dedicated to providing helpful resources. This included a list of autism apps and advocacy and information resources like Family Outreach, Danny's Wish, Autism Navigator, Association for Science in Autism Treatment (ASAT), Council of Parent Attorneys and Advocates, Inc. (COPAA), and Autism Society. We also discussed federal/government-funded organizations like the Early Childhood Technical Assistance Center (ECTA), IRIS Center, Center for Parent Information and Resources (CPIR), and the Center on Technology and Disability.

With the conclusion of this chapter, we provided a holistic approach to supporting your child, encompassing not only direct strategies and techniques but also broader therapies and resource options.

In the next and final section, we will bring together all the knowledge and understanding gained so far, and provide a concluding note on the journey of aiding your child's development.

EACH STEP IS A POSITIVE PART OF THE PATH

Congratulations on completing this journey through the book! Your dedication and effort to better understand and support your child's unique developmental needs are truly commendable. By navigating through the chapters, absorbing the content, and exploring the various resources, strategies, and therapies, you've taken significant steps toward becoming an even more effective ally and advocate for your child.

Remember, every child is unique and so is their journey with autism. The tools and knowledge you've gained from this book should serve as a guide to help you and your child navigate this path. It's important to continue learning, adapting, and growing as your child does the same.

Again, well done on your progress, and thank you for your commitment to this vital cause. Your child is lucky to have such a dedicated and caring individual in their corner. We hope this book has been a valuable resource in your journey and will continue to serve as a reference in the days to come.

As we move forward, we'll enter the final section of the book, the conclusion. It's here that we'll weave together the various threads we've explored so far. We'll revisit the key insights, techniques, and therapies you've learned, creating a comprehensive tapestry that reflects your enriched understanding of autism and the many ways to foster growth and connection.

This conclusion will serve as a recap of the knowledge you've gained and as a springboard for continued learning and growth. It's your take-off point for applying what you've learned, tailoring strategies to your unique situation, and exploring even more resources and opportunities to support your child's development.

You've come so far, and we applaud your dedication. It's time to gather up these threads of understanding and carry them into your daily life. We're confident that you, armed with this knowledge and your unyielding love for your child, will make a world of difference in their life and yours.

CONCLUSION

As we close this comprehensive guide on navigating autism, let's revisit our journey together. This book aims to equip you with a deeper understanding of autism, its challenges, and the multitude of approaches available to address them. Through the lens of patience, love, and respect, we've unfolded an array of strategies that aim to manage and empower your child on their unique journey.

This concise conclusion refreshes the key ideas and lessons we've covered, reiterating their importance and practical applications. Let's take a moment to reflect on the insights you've gathered, the tools you've acquired, and the progress you're about to make.

Ready to summarize and synthesize everything we've learned? Let's embark on this final phase of our shared exploration.

This book has been a journey through the world of autism, beginning with an understanding of what autism is and how it is diagnosed. We've explored the many faces of autism, highlighting that it is a spectrum condition, with no two individuals experiencing it the same way. We've stressed the importance of early detection and intervention, underlining that it can be crucial to a child's development and long-term prospects.

We delved into the complexities of communication, breaking it down into expressive and receptive aspects. We unpacked the unique challenges faced by children with autism in these areas, and demonstrated practical methods to support their growth and development.

Behavioral challenges, a common concern for parents, were examined closely. We looked at the underlying reasons for these behaviors and offered effective strategies to help manage and reduce them. We also talked about how we could turn these challenges into opportunities for learning and growth.

Teaching skills, an integral part of helping your child navigate the world around them, were discussed at length. We highlighted vital skills like social, life, and academic skills, providing practical tips and strategies to help your child learn and grow in these areas.

We took a detailed look at expressive and receptive communication, emphasizing how communication goes beyond words and plays a significant role in the child's ability to express themselves and understand others. We also highlighted how children with autism might express themselves differently and why it's essential to support them in finding their unique modes of expression.

The chapter on expanding your toolkit introduced you to a wide array of therapies and resources to further support your child's development. We understood that a holistic approach, incorporating behavior-based, developmental, and socio-relational methods, can provide the most beneficial results.

The core takeaway from this information is that every child with autism has unique abilities, challenges, and potential. With patience, understanding, and the right strategies, we can create an environment that enables them to thrive. This book has equipped you with a toolbox filled with practical strategies and an understanding of autism that will help you support your child effectively. This knowledge and these tools are interlinked, each playing a part in the larger picture of your child's growth and development.

NEXT STEPS

As we reach the end of this book, I want to leave you with a call to action. Raising a child with autism can be challenging, but remember, it's not just a challenge, but a journey filled with opportunities for growth and learning. You can make a significant, meaningful difference in your child's life with patience, love, and the tools you've acquired from this book.

Remember, progress may not always be as quick or as linear as you'd like. It's essential to take it one step at a time, to celebrate even the smallest victories, and never to give up hope. Your resilience and tenacity can create an environment of support and understanding your child needs to thrive.

If this book has aided you in understanding and navigating your journey with autism, I invite you to leave a review or feedback on Amazon. Your thoughts and experiences can help other parents and caregivers in their own journeys. Moreover, if you found the information helpful, consider sharing it with friends or family members who may also benefit from these insights.

You are not alone on this journey; the strength of shared experiences and knowledge can make all the difference. Let's continue to support each other and celebrate the unique, valuable individuals that our children are.

A FINAL NOTE FROM THE AUTHOR

As the final pages of this book come to a close, I'd like to extend a personal note of encouragement and solidarity to you. As the parent or caregiver of a child with autism, you have embarked on a road that is both challenging and rewarding in ways beyond description. I've walked a similar path, and I want you to know that the strength you carry within you, the love you have for your child, and your dedication to understanding them better is commendable and inspiring.

This book was written from my heart, combining personal experience with scientific research, to help you navigate your unique experiences. I hope the strategies and insights provided will serve as a helpful guide, offering you support when the road gets rocky, a light in the dark when you're unsure of your next steps, and a reminder to celebrate the milestones, no matter how small they may seem.

Remember, every step you take is a testament to your resilience and the incredible love you have for your child. Each day, you're making a difference, even when it doesn't feel like it. You are doing a wonderful job.

As you continue on this path, know that you are not alone. There's a community out here ready to lend an ear, share experiences, and offer a helping hand. You are a part of this community, and together, we can continue to learn, grow, and create more inclusive, understanding spaces for our children.

I wish you all the best as you continue on your journey. Here's to many more victories, big and small, to shared stories of progress, and to the unwavering hope that binds us all. Good luck, and remember to always keep going, keep loving, and keep believing.

ABOUT THE AUTHOR

Morgan Stone is a mom who's lived the journey you're about to embark upon. When her own child was diagnosed with autism, Morgan found herself standing where you are now, filled with fear, confusion, and a desperate desire to find a way to connect with her child.

Rather than let the diagnosis define her child's future, Morgan set out on a mission to find the most effective and practical strategies to help her child thrive. She devoted years of her life to researching, learning, and experimenting with different approaches. In the process, she discovered a unique 5-step strategy that made an enormous difference in her child's development and their family life.

Over the years, Morgan's approach has been shared and used by other parents in her community, who have reported similar improvements. Her practical, hands-on approach resonated with them, and they found the same success using her simple methods.

So, this isn't a book written by an academic or a clinician, but a real parent who's lived the ASD journey and found practical solutions that worked for her family. It's this real-world experience, this tried-and-tested knowledge, and this deep empathy and understanding for what you're going through, that makes Morgan the perfect guide on your road ahead.

In this book, Morgan shares the wisdom she's gained from her personal journey, providing you with the tools and insights she wishes she had when her family received their diagnosis. It's her hope that this book will serve as a beacon for you, helping to light your path as you navigate the challenges and joys of raising a child with ASD.

Before Morgan discovered and utilized the methods she shares in this book, the road was long, winding, and fraught with obstacles. The vast amount of information, different treatments, and approaches available for autism were overwhelming and often conflicting. Each day was a struggle, a battle against uncertainty and desperation.

Morgan experienced first-hand the stress of tirelessly researching every night, attending countless therapy sessions, and navigating the labyrinth of medical jargon and educational plans. She understood the heartache of not being able to connect with her child, of not knowing how to help him thrive in a world that seemed so ill-prepared for him.

Even the simple task of finding out where to start was a huge one, as was sifting through the conflicting advice of well-meaning friends, family, and professionals. She was all too familiar with the countless sleepless nights, the constant worry, and the unending questions about the future.

Morgan's initial journey was marked by trial and error, by missteps and breakthroughs. It took her years to find the right combination of strategies that resonated with her child and benefited her family.

Her simple approach, outlined in this book, has turned her struggle into a roadmap for success for parents like you. The journey to the result promised in this book was hard-won, but it need not be so for you. With the insights and strategies contained in these pages, your path can be more straightforward and less stressful.

If you're a parent seeking not just understanding, but also practical and effective strategies to support your child with ASD, then this book is written with you in mind. This is not a textbook penned by distant academics, but a practical guide authored by a parent who has walked the path you're embarking on, who has faced the same fears and worries you're grappling with now.

This book is for those who feel overwhelmed by a sea of complex medical terms, jargon-filled articles, and well-intended advice that only seems to confuse more than clarify. It's for those yearning for a clear, easy-to-follow strategy that's rooted in real-world experience and genuine success.

This book is for you if you're ready to replace feelings of confusion and anxiety with a sense of empowerment and confidence. If you're committed to giving your child the best possible start, building a strong connection with them, and helping them reach their full potential, then you're holding the right book.

Your journey with ASD might be challenging, and at times, it may feel as though you're navigating uncharted waters. But with this book as your guide, you can journey forth knowing you're not alone and that a proven path to a more hopeful future is laid out before you. You've taken the first step by picking up this book, and that's a testament to your determination and love for your child.

So take a deep breath, hold on tight to your courage and hope. You're about to embark on a transformative journey. One that will empower you to become not just your child's parent, but their most effective advocate, their pillar of support, and their guiding light.

www.ingramcontent.com/pod-product-compliance
Lightning Source LLC
Chambersburg PA
CBHW050811260726
48660CB00004B/1373